James Brilliant is a financial services regulatory lawyer and partner in an international asset management firm.

He has held senior legal and compliance positions in the financial sector since 2012. Before that, he was in private practice at Fred Philpott's chambers in Gough Square and then law firms Shearman & Sterling and Kirkland & Ellis.

City Limits

FCA Compliance for Financial Businesses

2nd Edition

City Limits

FCA Compliance for Financial Businesses

2nd Edition

James Brilliant
MA (Oxon)
Barrister (Inner Temple)

Law Brief Publishing

Published 2022 by Law Brief Publishing, an imprint of Law Brief Publishing Ltd
30 The Parks
Minehead
Somerset
TA24 8BT

www.lawbriefpublishing.com

Paperback: 978-1-914608-38-4

For my parents, Anna and Robin; for Lynne;
and in loving memory of Rod.

"… nil posse creari de nihilo…" (Lucretius)

CONTENTS

1 INTRODUCTION

1.1 About this Book

This book is about compliance with the rules, guidance and directions of the UK's Financial Conduct Authority ("**FCA**"). It aims to highlight the financial regulatory topics likely to be of greatest relevance to the bulk of UK financial businesses and to present key requirements in a way that is accessible for anyone who is tasked with advising on or overseeing compliance with those requirements.

The archetypal "financial business" contemplated in this book is a UK-headquartered, FCA solo-regulated "investment firm" which carries on certain advisory, intermediary, execution or portfolio management activities as further described in §3.2.1. Consideration is also given to "alternative investment fund managers" (§3.2.2) and "credit firms" (§3.2.3). Other types of financial business are likely to be subject to many of the same, or similar, high-level requirements, but supplemented by specific legislation or specialist regimes which are beyond the scope of this book.

Terms defined in the FCA Handbook Glossary have the same meanings in this book. For some of those terms, summaries of the definitions are given in this book for convenience; those summaries are subject to the full definitions as given in the FCA Handbook Glossary. A list of abbreviations used in this book is set out in §2.

All publications referenced are published by the FCA unless otherwise specified. These include webpages and "documents" (such as Dear CEO Letters, templates and notes), where the year of publication given is the "last updated" year if applicable. Other types of FCA publication include Consultation Paper ("**CP**"), Discussion Paper ("**DP**"), Finalised Guidance ("**FG**"), Feedback Statement ("**FS**"), Policy Statement ("**PS**") and Thematic Review ("**TR**"), where, in each case, the first two digits of the reference number are the publication year.

Information in this book is intended to represent law and practice as at 1 January 2022.

1.2 The FCA: From Big Bang to Twin Peaks

The UK's financial regulatory framework exists to protect society from the devastating harm that can be done to personal, corporate and public finances by the unscrupulous, incompetent or unfair behaviour of those providing financial services or participating in the financial markets.

A classic hallmark of any regulatory framework is superintendence by an executive branch agency, whose purpose is traditionally perceived as being to issue rules and guidance, impose licensing regimes and ongoing operating conditions, and intervene and penalise in cases of non-compliance. This layer of administration is subordinated to the ultimate jurisdiction of the courts to adjudicate in case of dispute or criminal proceedings.

In the case of financial services in the UK, the conduct regulator for all 58,000 or so firms within the sector is the FCA. For over 95% of those firms (more than 56,000 "solo-regulated" firms), the FCA is responsible also for authorisation and prudential supervision. The remaining firms are the larger, "dual-regulated", institutions – banks, building societies, credit unions, insurers and designated investment firms – which, while still conduct-regulated by the FCA, are authorised and prudentially regulated by the Prudential Regulation Authority ("**PRA**"). The PRA is a subsidiary of the Bank of England, and its relationship with the FCA is governed by a Memorandum of Understanding which notes that the two authorities "*have separate and independent mandates, which are set out in statute, reflecting the UK's 'Twin Peaks' micro-regulatory system*".[1] It is FCA rather than PRA authorisation and regulation that are the subject of this book.

1 "Memorandum of Understanding: Between the Financial Conduct Authority and the Bank of England (exercising its prudential regulation functions)" (FCA and PRA, 2019).

The FCA in its current form has existed since 2013, but its origins as an independent statutory financial regulator can be traced back to the 1980s. Under Margaret Thatcher's Conservative government, various restrictive practices in the UK financial markets were rapidly abolished, enabling domestic and global players to scale up their operations in the City during what came to be called the "Big Bang". To encourage such investment, the Government sought to promote confidence in the UK financial system and established the Securities and Investments Board ("**SIB**") under the Financial Services Act 1986 (which commenced in 1988).

The main role of the SIB initially was to oversee the five self-regulatory organisations ("**SROs**") in existence at that time, which covered futures broking and dealing, financial intermediation, investment management, life assurance broking and securities broking. The SROs represented the culmination of a 700-year-old tradition of statutory self-regulation in the City that stretched back to 1285, when the Court of Aldermen was first authorised by a statute of Edward I to license brokers and prosecute unlicensed brokers.

Several financial scandals in the 1990s spelled the end for the SROs altogether. Widespread mis-selling of various personal savings plans, as well as misconduct at the Maxwell company pension funds and Barings Bank, fuelled criticism that the system of SROs was not delivering adequate standards of investor protection or supervision, was confusing for investors, lacked accountability, was unsuited to a new reality where the distinctions between different types of financial institution and their products were increasingly blurred, and was not structured appropriately to regulate multinational firms effectively.[2]

In response, Tony Blair's incoming Labour administration changed the SIB's name to the Financial Services Authority ("**FSA**") and then gradually set about transforming the FSA into a unitary conduct and prudential regulator constituted under the Financial Services and

---

2 C. Blair, "Financial Services and Markets Bill [Bill 121 of 1998-99]" (Research Paper 99/68) (House of Commons Library, 1999).

Markets Act 2000 ("**FSMA**"). The transition was formally completed in 2001 with the commencement of FSMA.

This single-regulator set-up lasted a little more than a decade. Its most serious challenges came during the 2008 global financial crisis, which brought to the fore a perceived "regulatory underlap" whereby "*no single institution has the responsibility, authority or powers to monitor the system as a whole, identify potentially destabilising trends, and respond to them with concerted action*".[3]

Thus in 2013 the FSA was renamed and recast as the FCA; the more systemically important part of its micro-prudential supervisory remit was hived off to the PRA while other organs of the Bank of England received newly-created macro-prudential responsibilities and certain other supervisory functions. This restructuring was achieved formally by amending FSMA through the Financial Services Act 2012.

Notable organisational reforms of the FCA since 2013 include: taking over responsibility for regulating the consumer credit industry from the Office of Fair Trading in 2014; establishing the Payment Systems Regulator as a subsidiary in 2015; and, since 2017, phasing out the term "UK Listing Authority" to refer to the FCA's primary market functions of monitoring market disclosures, reviewing and approving prospectuses and operating the UK listing regime.

The FCA is a creature of statute whose genetic code has lengthened considerably over time. When it was the SIB, its specifications were contained in six concise paragraphs in Schedule 7 to the Financial Services Act 1986. Today's regulator, by contrast, is endowed with a wide set of mandates and powers rooted in a catalogue of "general functions", "general duties", "strategic and operational objectives", "regulatory principles" (also referred to by the FCA as the "principles of good

3 "A new approach to financial regulation: judgement, focus and stability" (HM Treasury, 2010).

regulation") and other similar strictures laid out in the opening 20 sections of FSMA and a further 27 paragraphs in Schedule 1ZA.[4]

This expansion has driven a broadening in the overall aim of the FCA, which is (in its own words) to "*add public value by improving how financial markets operate, to benefit individuals, businesses and the UK economy*".[5]

Consistent with this, the FCA has moved beyond simply fulfilling a rule-making mandate, towards occupying a position from which it seeks to influence the behaviour of firms through a range of techniques including nudges and thought leadership. As its Chief Executive said in 2018: "*In the traditional world of regulation, rules act as prescriptive statements that forbid, require or permit some action or outcome... The problem is that in practice a set of rules tends to underdetermine what needs to be done... So, to the verbs of forbidding, requiring and permitting, I would add enabling, encouraging and incentivising as important tasks of the regulator*".[6]

These incremental shifts in both remit and supervisory tone are nowhere more evident than on the FCA's website, which today carries essays, speeches, blogs and podcasts that go beyond the confines of conduct in financial intermediation, and respond to deeper questions about environmental sustainability, social purpose, diversity and inclusion, artificial intelligence and the ethical use of big data. The FCA is clear in

---

4 The FCA's "strategic objective" is ensuring that the relevant markets function well, and its "operational objectives" are the "consumer protection objective", the "integrity objective" and the "competition objective" (FSMA s. 1B(2), (3)). The "principles of good regulation" come under the headings of "efficiency and economy", "proportionality", sustainable growth", "consumer responsibility", "senior management responsibility", "recognising the differences in the businesses carried on by different regulated persons", "openness and disclosure" and "transparency" (FSMA s. 3B(1); "Principles of good regulation" (webpage, 2016)).

5 "Our Mission 2017 – How we regulate financial services" (document, 2017).

6 A. Bailey, "The role of regulation in encouraging good culture" (speech, Investment Association Culture Conference, Mansion House, London, 06/11/2018).

its ambitions to play a type of active – even activist – role in trying to shape public policy that came less naturally to its predecessors. This is the stance of a regulator that keenly feels the weight of its responsibilities for an industry that employs over 2.2 million people in the UK and contributes £65.6bn in tax each year – and whose failure can, as the FCA Chair observed in 2018 when reflecting on the tenth anniversary of the Lehman collapse, lead to "*tragedies of individual loss: loss of employment, loss of savings, loss of mental or physical health and, in some cases, loss of life*".[7]

1.3 The FCA Handbook

The FCA's "general functions" under FSMA include formulating rules, codes, guidance and general policy and principles,[8] and its powers to do so are contained in Part 9A.

The FCA makes its rules by "rule-making instrument", all of which are reproduced in the FCA's Handbook of rules and guidance ("**FCA Handbook**") which is freely available online. Technically the definitive versions of the FCA rules are the original instruments themselves.[9]

In the FCA Handbook, the rules are marked "R". Other legislative provisions include evidential provisions ("E"), guidance ("G"), directions ("D"), principles ("P") and descriptions of conduct ("C"). There are also excerpts and copy-outs from UK legislation which are marked with "UK" or a UK flag.

7 C. Randell, "Ten years after Lehman: how accountants can make finance safer" (speech, ICAEW Canary Wharf Members' Club, 06/09/2018).

8 FSMA s. 1B(6).

9 "Reader's Guide: An introduction to the Handbook" (document, 2021).

The provisions of the FCA Handbook are organised primarily in 50 "modules" which are thematically grouped together in nine "blocks".[10] Constructed on an epic scale, just three of the more prominent modules – SUP, SYSC and COBS – alone occupy more than 2,800 pages. To complicate matters further, a labyrinthine network of cross-references and densely-defined technical terms runs through the whole corpus.

The size and complexity of the FCA Handbook are the result of two main structural factors.

Firstly, the FCA Handbook caters to the needs of myriad kinds of financial businesses differentiated by various criteria such as regulated activity, client type, financial resources, group structure and so on. The FCA Handbook Glossary has entries for around 130 different varieties of firm, from "AIFM" to "venture capital firm". FCA provisions often need to have the firms in scope spelled out at great length, meaning that firms effectively must chisel out a tailored version of the FCA Handbook in order to isolate the provisions that apply to them specifically.

Secondly, multiple legislative rivers and tributaries drain into the basin of UK financial services regulation. These include:

- measures promulgated by the FCA using its statutory powers;
- legal and regulatory obligations that are contained in UK acts of Parliament and statutory instruments;
- a large body of onshored regulations originating in EU regulations which were formerly directly applicable in the UK by virtue of its membership of the EU, and becoming part of

---

10 The nine blocks are: High Level Standards; Prudential Standards; Business Standards; Regulatory Processes; Redress; Specialist sourcebooks; Listing, Prospectus and Disclosure; Handbook Guides; and Regulatory Guides.

UK domestic law as soon as the Brexit implementation period ended at 11pm on 31 December 2020;[11]

- non-legislative material produced by the EU and still considered relevant in principle by the FCA notwithstanding the UK's withdrawal from the EU;[12] and
- case law that includes judicial interpretation of statutory and regulatory provisions.

Rules may sometimes be time-limited, or temporary provisions may allow firms to choose which of two or more regimes to follow. For example, to help firms adapt to new requirements following Brexit, the FCA was empowered to make certain "transitional directions" which, as made, generally apply until 31 March 2022 and allow firms to continue to comply with pre-existing requirements in specified areas until then.[13] Meanwhile, during the ongoing Covid-19 pandemic, forbearance and other temporary changes in regulatory expectations have routinely been communicated at short notice through the FCA website and not reflected in the FCA Handbook at all (see §5.5).

The overall result is that a firm using the FCA Handbook to construct a compliance programme must be sensitive to the many technical definitions, cross-references, exceptions, redundancies and other

---

11 European Union (Withdrawal) Act 2018 ss. 1A, 3. The onshoring process for EU regulations typically involved introducing domestic "amending" regulations at the same time "*to prevent, remedy or mitigate (a) any failure of retained EU law to operate effectively, or (b) any other deficiency in retained EU law, arising from the withdrawal of the United Kingdom from the EU*" (s. 8). For example, the effective onshoring of MiFIR and MiFID Org Reg was enabled by the Markets in Financial Instruments (Amendment) (EU Exit) Regulations 2018, which amended the retained EU regulations by replacing references to EU legislation and institutions with their UK equivalents.

12 "Brexit: our approach to EU non-legislative materials" (document, 2020).

13 Financial Services and Markets Act 2000 (Amendment) (EU Exit) Regulations 2019 r. 198(1); "Onshoring and the Temporary Transitional Power" (webpage, 2020).

subtleties which pervade its provisions. The FCA acknowledges that, for many firms, it may take "*significant effort to navigate and interpret our Handbook, necessitating expenditure and reliance on external professional services*", and that implementing rules in a manual way creates, specifically, "*the risk of different interpretations and inconsistent reporting*".[14]

If Euclid once counselled Ptolemy I that there was no royal road to geometry, he might have said the same for FCA compliance. The FCA has signalled a desire for such a road to be built, and is sponsoring work programmes under its "RegTech" banner to harness "*technology that drives efficiencies by closing the gap between intention and interpretation*" and possibly achieve "*a more interactive FCA Handbook better tailored to the firm's permissions [that] could make compliance and reporting requirements clearer*".[15] In the meantime, it is hoped that this book might prove a useful navigational aid for those plotting a course through the UK financial regulatory landscape.

James Brilliant
January 2022

---

14 "Digital Regulatory Reporting – Feedback Statement on Call for Input" (FS18/2).

15 "Call for input on supporting the development and adopters of RegTech" (FS16/4).

2 ABBREVIATIONS

2.1 Regulatory and Legislative Provisions

The following abbreviations refer to the corresponding provisions, as amended.

2.1.1 FCA Handbook Modules

APER	Statements of Principle and Code of Practice for Approved Persons
CASS	Client Assets
COBS	Conduct of Business Sourcebook
COCON	Code of Conduct for Staff sourcebook
COLL	Collective Investment Schemes
CONC	Consumer Credit sourcebook
COND	Threshold Conditions
DEPP	Decision Procedure and Penalties Manual
DISP	Dispute Resolution: Complaints
DTR	Disclosure Guidance and Transparency Rules sourcebook

FCG	Financial Crime Guide: A firm's guide to countering financial crime risks
FCTR	Financial Crime Thematic Reviews
FEES	Fees Manual
FIT	Fit and Proper test for Employees and Senior Personnel
GENPRU	General Prudential sourcebook
IFPRU	Prudential sourcebook for Investment Firms
IPRU-INV	Interim Prudential sourcebook for Investment Businesses
M2G	The MiFID 2 Onshoring Guide
MAR	Market Conduct
MCOB	Mortgages and Home Finance: Conduct of Business sourcebook
MIFIDPRU	Prudential sourcebook for MiFID Investment Firms
PERG	The Perimeter Guidance Manual
PRIN	Principles for Businesses
PROD	Product Intervention and Product Governance Sourcebook

RPPD	The Responsibilities of Providers and Distributors for the Fair Treatment of Customers
SUP	Supervision
SYSC	Senior Management Arrangements, Systems and Controls
TC	Training and Competence
UNFCOG	The Unfair Contract Terms and Consumer Notices Regulatory Guide

2.1.2 Onshored Regulations

AIFMD Level 2 Regulation	UK version of Commission Delegated Regulation (EU) 231/2013
Benchmarks Regulation	UK version of Regulation (EU) 2016/1011
CRR or UK CRR	UK version of Regulation (EU) 575/2013
EMIR	UK version of Regulation (EU) 648/2012
EMIR Delegated Regulation	UK version of Commission Delegated Regulation (EU) 149/2013

EMIR Implementing Regulation	UK version of Commission Implementing Regulation (EU) 1247/2012
GDPR	UK version of Regulation (EU) 2016/679
Insider Lists ITS	UK version of Commission Implementing Regulation (EU) 2016/347
MA Reg	UK version of Regulation (EU) 596/2014
MA Reg Delegated Regulation	UK version of Commission Delegated Regulation (EU) 2016/522
MA Reg ITS	UK version of Commission Implementing Regulation (EU) 2016/347
MA Reg RTS	UK version of Commission Delegated Regulation (EU) 2016/957
MiFID Org Regulation	UK version of Commission Delegated Regulation (EU) 2017/565
MiFID RTS 1	UK version of Commission Delegated Regulation (EU) 2017/587
MiFID RTS 2	UK version of Commission Delegated Regulation (EU) 2017/583
MiFID RTS 22	UK version of Commission Delegated Regulation (EU) 2017/590

MiFID RTS 27	UK version of Commission Delegated Regulation (EU) 2017/575
MiFID RTS 28	UK version of Commission Delegated Regulation (EU) 2017/576
MiFIR	UK version of Regulation (EU) 600/2014
MiFIR Delegated Regulation	UK version of Commission Delegated Regulation (EU) 2017/567
PRIIPs Regulation	UK version of Regulation (EU) 1286/2014
PRIIPs KID RTS	UK version of Commission Delegated Regulation (EU) 2017/653
Securitisation Regulation	UK version of Regulation (EU) 2017/2402
SFTR	UK version of Regulation (EU) 2015/2365
Short Selling Regulation	UK version of Regulation (EU) 236/2012

2.1.3 **Other UK Legislation**

AIFM Regulations	Alternative Investment Fund Managers Regulations 2013
CCA	Consumer Credit Act 1974

FSMA	Financial Services and Markets Act 2000
FSMA RAO	Financial Services and Markets Act 2000 (Regulated Activities) Order 2001
MLR	Money Laundering, Terrorist Financing and Transfer of Funds (Information on the Payer) Regulations 2017
PECR	Privacy and Electronic Communications (EC Directive) Regulations 2003

2.1.4 EU Directives

AIFMD	Alternative Investment Fund Managers Directive 2011/61/EU
MiFID, MiFID 2 or MiFID II	Recast Markets in Financial Instruments Directive 2014/65/EU
MiFID I	Markets in Financial Instruments Directive 2004/39/EU
MiFID Delegated Directive	Commission Delegated Directive (EU) 2017/593
Solvency II Directive	Solvency II Directive 2009/138/EC
UCITS Directive	UCITS Directive 2009/65/EC (as amended, notably, by UCITS V Directive 2014/91/EU)

2.2 Public Bodies

EBA	European Banking Authority
ESMA	European Securities and Markets Authority
FCA	Financial Conduct Authority
ICO	Information Commissioner's Office
PRA	Prudential Regulation Authority
TCFD	Task Force on Climate-related Financial Disclosures

PART A

SUPERVISORY PROCESSES

3 FCA AUTHORISATION

3.1 Who Needs to be Authorised by the FCA?

The obligation on financial businesses to obtain regulatory authorisation is encapsulated in the "**general prohibition**" which is set out in FSMA s. 19(1):

> *No person may carry on a regulated activity in the United Kingdom, or purport to do so, unless he is –*
>
> *(a) an authorised person; or*
>
> *(b) an exempt person.*

Contravention of the general prohibition is a criminal offence under FSMA s. 23(1), and certain agreements done with or through unauthorised persons may be rendered unenforceable under ss. 26 or 27 respectively.

"**Regulated activities**" are activities which have been specified as such in an order made by HM Treasury and are carried on by way of business.[16] The relevant order prescribing the regulated activities is FSMA RAO, which is considered further in §3.2.

The carve-out for "**exempt persons**" encompasses, notably, unauthorised firms operating as "**appointed representatives**" under the contractual responsibility of an authorised principal in accordance with FSMA s. 39. Other, relatively narrow, classes of exempt persons are set out in the

---

16 FSMA s. 22. Circumstances in which persons are, or are not, to be regarded as "**carrying on regulated activities by way of business**" are defined in the Financial Services and Markets Act 2000 (Carrying on Regulated Activities by Way of Business) Order 2001 and also the subject of PERG 2.3.

Financial Services and Markets Act 2000 (Exemption) Order 2001.[17] Unless exempt, any person wishing to conduct regulated activities in the UK is required to be authorised.

UK-based firms requiring authorisation must apply to the FCA or PRA for regulatory permission, which is governed by Part 4A of FSMA and consequently known as "**Part 4A permission**".[18] The majority of financial firms must apply to the FCA (rather than the PRA) for Part 4A permission, including investment firms, AIFMs and credit firms (as defined in §3.2). PRA Part 4A permission must be sought by banks, building societies, credit unions, insurers and designated investment firms,[19] and is beyond the scope of this book.

3.2 Regulated Activities

Under FSMA RAO art. 4, the regulated activities are those specified in FSMA RAO Parts 2, 3A and 3B.

Of the regulated activities specified in FSMA RAO Part 2, most are caught only when carried on in relation to the "**specified investments**" listed in FSMA RAO Part 3.[20] The remainder are caught when carried on in relation to property of any kind.[21]

Detailed guidance on the scope of regulated activities is contained in PERG 2.7 (Activities: a broad outline), PERG 2.8 (Exclusions applicable to certain regulated activities) and PERG 2.9 (Regulated activities:

---

17 For relevant FCA guidance, see PERG 2.10 (Persons carrying on regulated activities who do not need authorisation) and PERG 2.11 (Persons who are exempt for credit-related regulated activities).

18 FSMA s. 55A.

19 Financial Services and Markets Act 2000 (PRA-regulated Activities) Order 2013.

20 For FCA guidance on the scope of specified investments, see PERG 2.6 (Specified investments: a broad outline).

21 These activities are broadly to do with investment funds and pension schemes and are conveniently listed at PERG 2.5.1-AG.

exclusions applicable to certain circumstances). There is also relevant material in PERG 8 (Financial promotion and related activities).

While some provisions of the FCA Handbook apply in whole or in part to every authorised firm, a great many others are applicable only to certain types of firm which carry out a defined range of financial activities. Summarised below are outlines of those which feature most prominently in this book.

3.2.1 Investment Firms

An "**investment firm**" is defined as, essentially, "*any person whose regular occupation or business is the provision of one or more investment services to third parties and/or the performance of one or more investment activities on a professional basis*".

"**Investment services and/or activities**" are, in turn, defined as those listed in FSMA RAO Schedule 2 Part 3, insofar as they relate to any of the "**financial instruments**" as listed in FSMA RAO Schedule 2 Part 1:

Investment services and/or activities	**Financial instruments**
• Reception and transmission of orders in relation to one or more financial instruments • Execution of orders on behalf of clients • Dealing on own account	• Transferable securities • Money-market instruments • Units in collective investment undertakings • Options, futures, swaps, forward rate agreements and any other derivative contracts relating to securities, currencies, interest rates or yields, emission allowances or other derivatives instruments, financial

• Portfolio management • The making of a personal recommendation • Underwriting of financial instruments and/or placing of financial instruments on a firm commitment basis • Placing of financial instruments without a firm commitment basis • Operation of an MTF • Operation of an OTF	indices or financial measures which may be settled physically or in cash • Options, futures, swaps, forwards and any other derivative contracts relating to commodities that must be settled in cash or may be settled in cash at the option of one of the parties (other than by reason of a default or other termination event) • Options, futures, swaps, and any other derivative contract relating to commodities that can be physically settled provided that they are traded on a regulated market, an MTF, or an OTF, except for wholesale energy products traded on an OTF that must be physically settled • Option, futures, swaps, forwards and any other derivative contracts relating to commodities, that can be physically settled not otherwise mentioned immediately above and not being for commercial purposes, which have the characteristics of other derivative financial instruments • Derivative instruments for the transfer of credit risk • Financial contracts for differences • Options, futures, swaps, forward rate agreements and any other derivative contracts relating to climatic

	variables, freight rates or inflation rates or other official economic statistics that must be settled in cash or may be settled in cash at the option of one of the parties other than by reason of default or other termination event, as well as any other derivative contracts relating to assets, rights, obligations, indices and measures not otherwise mentioned in this Section, which have the characteristics of other derivative financial instruments, having regard to whether, inter alia, they are traded on a regulated market, OTF, or an MTF • Emission allowances consisting of any units recognised for compliance with the requirements of Directive 2003/87/EC (Emissions Trading Scheme) or allowances created under article 18 of the [Greenhouse Gas Emissions Trading Scheme Order 2020]

"Investment services and/or activities" and "financial instruments" are concepts which were originally introduced to the UK regulatory framework in 2007 in order to implement MiFID I (Annex I Sections A and C respectively). They were superimposed upon the pre-existing FSMA RAO schema of "regulated activities" and "specified investments" which had been in force since 2001.

The "MiFID-derived" and "native" sets of definitions fit together fairly neatly, such that a firm carrying on an "investment service and/or activity" requires regulatory authorisation to carry on one or more corresponding "regulated activities". There is detailed guidance in PERG

13 Annex 2 which shows, for example, that a firm carrying on the investment activity of "dealing on own account" needs permission to carry on the regulated activity of "dealing in investments as principal".

An investment firm that has its head office or registered office in the UK is by definition also a "**MiFID investment firm**", unless it is exempt because it is a "MiFID optional exemption firm"[22] or comes within a narrow range of other exemptions in FSMA RAO Schedule 3 Part 1. For ease of reference, the FCA sometimes refers to these exemptions as "**article 3**" and "**article 2**" exemptions respectively owing to their original location in MiFID.[23]

One important consequence of being a MiFID investment firm is that a firm must in principle comply with the regulatory provisions (addressed in this book) governing organisational, conduct and operational aspects of firms' businesses which originally derived from (or already gave effect to) MiFID.

MiFID investment firms should also note that they are prevented from relying on certain exclusions from regulation which are available under FSMA RAO to other types of firm, such as the exclusions for "absence of holding out" or "groups or joint enterprises". This is by virtue of the so-called "**MiFID override**" which is set out in FSMA RAO art. 4(4) and explained in PERG 2.5.5G.

---

22 "**MiFID optional exemption firms**" are investment firms that do not hold client money or assets, do not provide any investment service other than reception and transmission of orders or investment advice, or both, in relation to transferable securities and units in collective investment undertakings, and meet certain other conditions as described in M2G 2.1.1G and PERG 13.5 Q49. MiFID optional exemption firms are entitled to treat various MiFID-derived "systems and controls" rules as guidance only or, in some cases, to disapply them entirely, as set out at M2G 2.7.1G. The term refers to the FCA's power to exercise the exemption as contained in the Financial Services and Markets Act 2000 (Markets in Financial Instruments) Regulations 2017 r. 8.

23 PERG 13.5 Q35.

3.2.2 Alternative Investment Fund Managers

The regime for alternative investment fund managers ("**AIFMs**") originated in an EU directive – AIFMD – which was implemented in 2013 principally through the EU's AIFMD Level 2 Regulation, the UK's AIFM Regulations, and the FUND sourcebook.

An AIFM is a legal person whose regular business is managing one or more "**alternative investment funds**" ("**AIFs**").[24] An AIF, in turn, is defined as a collective investment undertaking which (1) raises capital from a number of investors, with a view to investing it in accordance with a defined investment policy for the benefit of those investors, and (2) is not a UK UCITS.[25]

"**Managing an AIF**" means performing at least risk management or portfolio management for the AIF,[26] and is a regulated activity under FSMA RAO art.51ZC. A UK-established AIFM with Part 4A permission to carry on such regulated activity is referred to as a "**UK AIFM**".

An AIFM whose portfolios of AIFs come within certain size thresholds[27] is a "**small AIFM**", and a UK AIFM that is a small AIFM may be either

---

24 AIFM Regulations r. 4(1).

25 AIFM Regulations r. 3(1).

26 AIFM Regulations r. 4(2).

27 Namely: the value of whose assets under management (a) does not exceed 500 million euros in total in cases where the portfolios of AIFs consist of AIFs that are unleveraged and have no redemption rights exercisable during a period of 5 years following the date of initial investment in each AIF; or (b) does not exceed 100 million euros in total in other cases, including any assets acquired through the use of leverage. (AIFM Regulations r.9(1).)

a "**small authorised UK AIFM**" or a "**small registered UK AIFM**".[28] All other UK AIFMs are "**full-scope UK AIFMs**".[29]

AIFMs are subject to various specific organisational and operational rules, many of which are set out in FUND 3 and summarised in §13.2. The bulk of those rules is largely disapplied for small AIFMs. There are also mandatory business restrictions that significantly impact the range of activities in which full-scope UK AIFMs can engage; these are set out in FUND 1.4.

There are detailed provisions on the scope of the AIFMs regime in PERG 16 (in addition to the general guidance in PERG 2).

Guidance on the authorisation process for AIFMs is set out in "UK AIFMs" (webpage, 2021).

3.2.3 Credit Firms

Over 70% of all FCA-authorised firms are "**credit firms**", which are firms that have permission to carry on a "**credit-related regulated activity**" as defined in FSMA RAO Parts 2 or 3A.[30]

---

28 FUND 1.3.5G. The conditions for registration as a small registered AIFM are set out in AIFM Regulations r. 10.

29 A small authorised UK AIFM may "opt up" to be treated as a full-scope UK AIFM, and a small registered UK AIFM may apply to become a small authorised UK AIFM or a full-scope UK AIFM. (FUND 1.3.6G(2), 1.3.8G.)

30 Namely, any of the following services, carried on by way of business and relating to a specified investment or (in the case of (j) and (k)) a person's financial standing: (a) entering into a regulated credit agreement as lender; (b) exercising, or having the right to exercise, the lender's rights and duties under a regulated credit agreement; (c) credit broking; (d) debt adjusting; (e) debt counselling; (f) debt collecting; (g) debt administration; (ga) advising on regulated credit agreements for the acquisition of land; (h) entering into a regulated consumer hire agreement as owner; (i) exercising, or having the right to exercise, the

Credit firms are subject to various specific organisational and operational rules, many of which are set out in the CCA and the CONC sourcebook and summarised in §13.3.

A subset of credit firms, termed "**limited permission**" firms, have permission only to carry on "**relevant credit activities**" as defined in FSMA Schedule 6 para. 2G. Relevant credit activities include consumer hire, certain credit broking where this is a secondary activity, and certain lending where this is a secondary activity and no interest or charges are applied. Limited permission firms benefit from a light-touch authorisation process including certain exemptions from the FCA's threshold conditions (considered in §3.3).[31]

Note that credit-related regulated activities are separate from activities in respect of "**home finance transactions**", which comprise regulated mortgage contracts, equity release transactions, home purchase plans, and

owner's rights and duties under a regulated consumer hire agreement; (j) providing credit information services; (k) providing credit references; (l) operating an electronic system in relation to lending, but (other than in FEES and SUP) only insofar as it relates to a borrower or prospective borrower under a P2P agreement; (m) agreeing to carry on a regulated activity so far as relevant to any of the activities in (a) to (l).

Note that the definition of "specified investment" includes "rights under a credit agreement" and "rights under a consumer hire agreement" (FSMA RAO arts.88D, 88E); "**credit agreement**" and "**consumer hire agreement**" are defined in FSMA RAO arts.60B and 60N respectively and considered further in §13.3.

For the activity of consumer credit debt counselling, there is detailed guidance on scope issues in PERG 17 (in addition to the material in PERG 2).

Finally, a firm that arranges cycle hire for its staff under a Government-promoted Cycle to Work scheme should consider whether the nature of the arrangements would inadvertently bring the firm within scope of credit broking – bearing in mind that there may be exemptions available to unregulated employers that are not available to those that are regulated. See "Cycle to Work Scheme – Guidance for Employers" (Department for Transport, 2019).

31 COND 1.1A.5AG(2).

regulated sale and rent back agreements. Operational requirements applicable specifically to home finance transactions are set out in MCOB.

3.3 FCA Authorisation Process

Firms applying to the FCA for Part 4A permission must do so in such manner as the FCA may direct.[32] The process includes using the FCA's Connect online system and an application fee is payable.[33] The amount of the fee varies by complexity, but, by way of indication, for most financial advisers, mortgage brokers and general insurance intermediaries it is £1,500.

In determining an application for Part 4A permission, the FCA must at a minimum ensure that the applicant will satisfy the "**threshold conditions**" which are specified in Schedule 6 to FSMA and COND, and organised under the following headings: "location of offices"; "effective supervision"; "appropriate resources"; "suitability"; and "business model".[34] This duty does not detract from the FCA's overall ability to take such steps as it considers necessary to advance its operational objectives.[35]

The FCA must determine the application within 6 months of receiving the completed application, or within 12 months of receiving an incomplete application.[36] The FCA has published further colour on the authorisation process in "FCA Mission: Approach to Supervision"

---

32 FSMA s. 55U(4)(a).

33 "Authorisation: what's involved" (webpage, 2021).

34 FSMA s. 55B(3).

35 FSMA s. 55V(4). The FCA's "**operational objectives**" are defined in FSMA s. 1B(3) as the "**consumer protection objective**", the "**integrity objective**" and the "**competition objective**", as defined in FSMA ss. 1C, 1D and 1E, respectively. For further colour, see "FCA Mission: Approach to Authorisation" (document, 2018).

36 FSMA s. 55V(1), (2).

(document, 2019). Where an applicant is aggrieved by a determination of the FCA, it may refer the matter to the Tribunal (see §6.3).[37]

Once authorised, firms are entered into the Financial Services Register, which is freely accessible online.

A firm must also ensure that, upon authorisation, it has in place appropriate SMF managers with requisite FCA approval, and any individuals performing FCA certification functions are duly certified, as discussed in §4.

3.4 FCA Rules and the Principles for Businesses

Once authorised, firms must comply with such rules "*(a) with respect to the carrying on by them of regulated activities, or (b) with respect to the carrying on by them of activities which are not regulated activities, as appear to the FCA to be necessary or expedient for the purpose of advancing one or more of its operational objectives*", which the FCA is empowered to make under FSMA s. 137A(1) – in other words, the FCA rules as reproduced in the FCA Handbook.

Of the FCA rules, first among equals are the Principles for Businesses ("**Principles**") set out at PRIN 2.1:

The Principles	
1 Integrity	A firm must conduct its business with integrity.
2 Skill, care and diligence	A firm must conduct its business with due skill, care and diligence.

[37] FSMA s. 55Z3(1).

3 Management and control	A firm must take reasonable care to organise and control its affairs responsibly and effectively, with adequate risk management systems.
4 Financial prudence	A firm must maintain adequate financial resources.
5 Market conduct	A firm must observe proper standards of market conduct.
6 Customers' interests	A firm must pay due regard to the interests of its customers and treat them fairly.
7 Communications with clients	A firm must pay due regard to the information needs of its clients, and communicate information to them in a way which is clear, fair and not misleading.
8 Conflicts of interest	A firm must manage conflicts of interest fairly, both between itself and its customers and between a customer and another client.
9 Customers: relationships of trust	A firm must take reasonable care to ensure the suitability of its advice and discretionary decisions for any customer who is entitled to rely upon its judgment.
10 Clients' assets	A firm must arrange adequate protection for clients' assets when it is responsible for them.
11 Relations with regulators	A firm must deal with its regulators in an open and cooperative way, and must disclose to the appropriate regulator appropriately anything relating to the firm of which that regulator would reasonably expect notice.

The special status of the Principles was articulated by Ouseley J in *R (British Bankers Association) v Financial Services Authority and others* [2011] EWHC 999 (Admin):

> *161. … The Principles are the overarching framework for regulation, for good reason. The FSA has clearly not promulgated, and has chosen not to promulgate, a detailed all-embracing comprehensive code of regulations to be interpreted as covering all possible circumstances… The overarching framework would always be in place to be the fundamental provision which would always govern the actions of the firms, as well as cover all those circumstances not provided for or adequately provided for by specific rules.*
>
> *162. The Principles are best understood as the ever present substrata to which the specific rules are added. The Principles always have to be complied with. The specific rules do not supplant them and cannot be used to contradict them. They are but specific applications of them to the particular requirements they cover…*

Non-compliance with a Principle can, on its own, provide the basis for FCA intervention.[38]

38 PRIN 1.1.7G.

4 SENIOR MANAGERS AND CERTIFICATION REGIME

4.1 Overview of SMCR

The senior managers and certification regime ("**SMCR**"), which takes effect through a combination of measures in FSMA and the FCA Handbook, was introduced for FCA solo-regulated firms in December 2019. It had earlier already come into force for banks and dual-regulated investment firms in March 2016 and insurers in December 2018. In each case, SMCR replaced the predecessor "approved persons" regime which had been in place since the commencement of FSMA in 2001.

According to the FCA, SMCR:

> *sets a new standard of conduct in financial services, ensuring:*
>
> - *greater personal accountability at all levels*
> - *minimum standards of conduct*
> - *staff in key jobs are fit and proper to perform their roles.*[39]

This is achieved through the following main components:[40]

---

[39] "Senior Managers and Certification Regime: solo-regulated firms" (webpage, 2020).

[40] For a more detailed overview table, see SYSC 23.3.

Component of SMCR	FSMA ref.	FCA Handbook ref.
Certain senior managers (known as "SMF managers") must: be assessed by firms for fitness and propriety; have a statement of responsibilities which can form the basis for personal liability; and be approved by the FCA.	ss. 59 to 63D	SUP 10C; SYSC 23 to 26
Staff performing certain functions (known as "FCA certification functions") must be assessed by firms for fitness and propriety and entered in the FCA Directory.	ss. 63E, 63F	SYSC 23, 27
Regulatory references must be requested as part of firms' fitness and propriety assessment.	N/A	SYSC 22
All staff, other than ancillary staff, must comply with the FCA's conduct rules in COCON.	ss. 64A to 64C	COCON

4.2 Types of SMCR Firm

Apart from an extremely limited set of exempt firms,[41] all FCA-authorised firms fall into one of three categories of "**SMCR firm**" – "enhanced scope", "limited scope" or "core" – as defined in SYSC 23 Annex 1:

- "**Enhanced scope SMCR firms**" include: significant SYSC firms;[42] CASS large firms;[43] firms satisfying certain "point in time" measurements;[44] firms satisfying certain "revenue measurements;[45] and other firms which have elected to be enhanced scope SMCR firms.[46]

- "**Limited scope SMCR firms**" include sole traders and certain types of consumer credit firms and claims management companies, among others, each to the extent that they have not

41 Such exempt firms are: overseas firms that do not have (and do not have an appointed representative that has) an establishment in the United Kingdom; EEA PTV firms that are pure reinsurers; TP UCITS qualifiers; TP AIFM qualifiers; and certain claims management firms coming within SYSC TP 8.2.1R (SYSC 23 Annex 1).

42 Defined in SYSC 1.5.2R.

43 Defined at CASS 1A.2.7R.

44 Namely: having assets under management of £50 billion or more as a 3-year rolling average, or 10,000 or more regulated mortgages outstanding at the latest reporting date.

45 Namely: firms with current total intermediary regulated business revenue of £35 million or more per annum calculated as a 3-year rolling average, or firms with annual revenue generated by regulated consumer credit lending of £100m or more calculated as a 3-year rolling average.

46 SYSC 23 Annex 1 Parts 7 to 11; opting up and opting back down are addressed in Part 12 and are effected by submitting Form O to the FCA.

elected to be enhanced scope SMCR firms or core SMCR firms.[47]

- "**Core SMCR firms**" are all remaining FCA-authorised firms which are not enhanced scope SMCR firms or limited scope SMCR firms.

Consequences of categorisation include the range of roles specified as being designated senior management functions (see §4.3.2), and the applicability of rules requiring responsibilities-related documentation to be maintained for SMF managers.[48]

4.3 SMF Managers

4.3.1 Designated Senior Management Functions

An FCA-authorised firm must take reasonable care to ensure that each person who "*performs a controlled function under an arrangement entered into by [that firm] in relation to the carrying on by [that firm] of a regulated activity*" is approved by the FCA.[49]

"**Controlled functions**" in this context are functions "*of a description specified in rules made by the FCA*".[50] "**Arrangement**" has a wide meaning encompassing "*any kind of arrangement for the performance of a function of [a firm] which is entered into by [that firm] or any contractor of his with another person", and including "that other person's appointment to an office, his becoming a partner or his employment (whether under a contract of service or otherwise)*".[51]

---

47 SYSC 23 Annex 1 Part 6; opting up and opting back down are addressed in Part 12 and are effected by submitting Form O to the FCA.

48 SYSC 23.3.3G.

49 FSMA s. 59(1).

50 FSMA s. 59(3)(b).

51 FSMA s. 59(10); SUP 10C.3.8G.

Controlled functions which the FCA is satisfied are senior management functions must be designated as such in FCA rules;[52] such functions are termed "**designated senior management functions**".[53]

Currently, the only controlled functions that have been specified by the FCA for authorised firms are the designated senior management functions. This means that, in principle, all authorised firms require FCA approval for a person if and only if that person is performing a designated senior management function under an arrangement with the firm.[54] Such persons, once approved by the FCA, are termed "**SMF managers**".

As a notable exception to this requirement, FCA approval is not needed for certain temporary arrangements. Under the "**12-week rule**", a firm may appoint an individual to provide cover for an SMF manager whose absence is temporary or reasonably unforeseen, for a period of less than 12 weeks in a consecutive 12-month period, without such cover amounting to the performance of a designated senior management function.[55]

---

52 FSMA s. 59(6A).

53 FSMA s. 59ZB. The FCA may determine that a function is a "**senior management function**" if, essentially, it requires the person performing it to be responsible for managing one or more aspects of the firm's affairs, so far as relating to a regulated activity, where those aspects involve or might involve a risk of serious consequences for the firm or for business or other interests in the United Kingdom (FSMA s. 59ZA(2)). "**Managing**" in this context includes taking decisions, or participating in the taking of decisions, about how one or more aspects of a firm's affairs should be carried on (FSMA s. 59ZA(3)).

54 SUP 10C.3.3G, 5G. Note that for appointed representatives – which are not authorised firms – a separate, less onerous regime exists, under which a different set of controlled functions (which are not designated senior management functions) is specified at SUP 10A.4.4R. This is a remnant of the predecessor "approved persons" regime which applied to authorised firms before SMCR.

55 SUP 10C.3.13R.

4.3.2 Specification of Designated Senior Management Functions

A full list of designated senior management functions is set out in the table at SUP 10C.4.3R and defined in SUP 10C.5 to 8A.

The subset of designated senior management functions which are relevant for a UK-headquartered core SMCR firm is set out at SUP 10C Annex 1 5.2R:[56]

FCA governing functions	**Summary**
SMF 1 (Chief executive function)	… having the responsibility, alone or jointly with one or more others, under the immediate authority of the governing body for the conduct of the whole of the business (or relevant activities) of the firm. (SUP 10C.5.22G)
SMF 3 (Executive director function)	… acting in the capacity of a director (other than a non-executive director) of the firm. (SUP 10C.5.1R)
SMF 9 (Chair of the governing body function)	… having responsibility for chairing, and overseeing the performance of the role of, the governing body of the firm. (SUP 10C.5A.7R)

56 For enhanced scope SMCR firms, see SUP 10C Annex 1 6.2R. For limited scope SMCR firms, see SUP 10C Annex 1 7.4R to 11G.

SMF 27 (Partner function)	... for an SMCR firm that is a partnership: being or occupying the position of a partner in that firm; or being or occupying the position of a partner in that firm (by whatever name called) AND acting as a member of the firm's governing body. (SUP 10C.5.14R)
FCA required functions	**Summary**
SMF 16 (Compliance oversight function)	... acting in the capacity of a person who is allocated the relevant function in applicable provisions of SYSC 3, SYSC 6, MiFID Org Regulation or AIFMD Level 2 Regulation. (SUP 10C.6.1R)
SMF 17 (Money laundering reporting function)	... acting in the capacity of the money laundering reporting officer of a firm, as appointed in accordance with applicable rules in SYSC 3 or SYSC 6. (SUP 10C.6.2R)

SUP 10C.3.4R includes the qualification that a function will only constitute a designated senior management function if it has first satisfied the prior conditions for being a "senior management function" – including the "management" and "risk of serious consequences" elements of that term's definition.[57] This is especially relevant to SMF 27 (Partner function), as it significantly narrows its scope and means that "*partners or*

[57] See footnote 53.

members who play no part in the management of the firm are unlikely to be performing the partner function".[58]

4.3.3 Procedure for Obtaining FCA Approval

An application for approval to perform a controlled function is submitted by a firm in respect of the candidate, following procedures made under FSMA s. 60 and set out in SUP 10C.10.

Key elements of the FCA approval process include:

- **Fitness and propriety.**

  Before applying for FCA approval, the firm must be satisfied that the candidate is a fit and proper person, having particular regard to whether the candidate: has obtained a qualification; has undergone, or is undergoing, training; possesses a level of competence; or has the personal characteristics, to the extent required by FCA rules.[59] This assessment must also include criminal records checks[60] as well as regulatory references (see §4.5.1).

  In assessing personal characteristics, the FCA has made it clear from various prohibition orders that a history of non-financial misconduct, and not just misconduct directly relevant to the provision of financial services, can impugn an individual's fitness and propriety. In recent years, individuals have been deemed to be not fit and proper for acts beyond the world of financial services including inducing individuals to breach

---

58 SUP 10C.5.18G.

59 FSMA s. 60A(1); SUP 10C.10.14G; FIT.

60 SUP 10C.10.16R. A firm must "*obtain the fullest information that it is lawfully able to obtain about the candidate under Part V of the Police Act 1997 (Certificates of Criminal Records, &c)*", which is a "standard" (as opposed to "basic" or "enhanced") check from the Disclosure and Barring Service (see Rehabilitation of Offenders Act 1974 (Exceptions) Order 1975, art. 3).

employment contracts, evading train fares, and drugs and sexual offences.[61] When evaluating non-financial misconduct, the Upper Tribunal has stated that regard should be had to the qualitative relevance of that conduct to the FCA's statutory objectives, as well as principles of proportionality and the right to a private life.[62]

- **Statements of responsibilities.**

An application for FCA approval should be accompanied by a statement of responsibilities about the candidate.[63] These must include any allocation to the candidate of the "**FCA-prescribed senior management responsibilities**" as defined in SYSC 24.2. Further guidance on statements of responsibilities is set out in SUP 10C.11, and the FCA also publishes statements of responsibilities for its own senior managers which reflect (to an extent) its expectations for regulated firms.[64]

Enhanced scope SMCR firms must, additionally, include handover procedures and materials[65] and management responsibilities maps.[66]

Limited scope SMCR firms are exempt from the requirement to allocate FCA-prescribed senior management responsibilities among SMF managers. However, they must instead comply

---

61 See final notices issued against Verrier (27/01/2014), Burrows (15/12/2014), Flowers (01/03/2018), and Jameson, Horsey and Cochran (each 03/11/2020).

62 *Jon Frensham v The Financial Conduct Authority* [2021] UKUT 0222 (TCC).

63 FSMA s. 60(2A); SUP 10C.10.11G.

64 "Senior Managers Regime" (document, 2021).

65 SUP 10C.10.13G; SYSC 25.9.

66 SUP 10C.10.13AD; SYSC 25.2.

with a broader requirement in SYSC 4.4 to apportion responsibilities among directors and senior managers.[67]

- **Submission of the application form.**

  Firms should submit the application for approval using Form A, shortened Form A or Form E depending on the candidate's previous approval status,[68] via the FCA's Connect online system. The FCA generally has three months from the time it receives a properly completed application in which to make its decision,[69] and may approve the application only if it is satisfied that the candidate is fit and proper (by reference to the criteria in FIT).[70]

  If a firm wishes to withdraw an application after it has been submitted (but prior to decision), it will need the consent of the candidate and any other relevant employer, and should use Form B.[71]

All approved persons are included in the Financial Services Register.

If the FCA decides to refuse an application for approval, or to grant the application subject to conditions or for a limited period (or both), the applicant firm or other interested party may refer the matter to the Tribunal (see §6.3).[72]

---

67 SYSC 23.3.3G.

68 SUP 10C.10.8D, 8AD and 9D.

69 FSMA s. 61(3A).

70 FSMA s. 61(1)(a); SUP 10C.10.32G.

71 FSMA s. 61(5); SUP 10C.10.36R.

72 FSMA s. 62.

4.3.4 Ongoing Obligations

Firms must comply with the following ongoing obligations in respect of their SMF managers:

- **Fitness and propriety**. A firm must consider the fitness and propriety of each SMF manager at least once a year and notify the FCA if there are any grounds on which the FCA could withdraw its approval.[73]

  Criminal records checks can be excluded from such repeat assessments,[74] and regulatory references are unlikely to be required.[75]

- **Statements of responsibilities**. A firm must, at all times, have a complete set of current statement of responsibilities for all its SMF managers.[76]

  Enhanced scope SMCR firms must, additionally, maintain adequate records of the steps taken to comply with the handover material rules,[77] and must at all times have a comprehensive and up-to-date management responsibilities map.[78]

- **Fresh applications to FCA**. FCA approval must be obtained before an SMF manager may move within a firm (using Form

---

73 FSMA s. 63(2A); SUP 10C.14.24G.

74 SUP 10C.10.23AG.

75 "The Senior Managers and Certification Regime: Guide for FCA solo-regulated firms" (document, 2019); SYSC 22.7.5G to 8G.

76 SUP 10C.11.20R.

77 SYSC 25.9.5R.

78 SYSC 25.2.1R(1).

E or (in some cases) Form A) [79] or between firms (using Form A or (in some cases) shortened Form A).[80]

- **Notifications to FCA.** A firm must notify the FCA if an SMF manager:

  - ceases to perform a designated senior management function (using Form C or (in some cases) qualified Form C or Form E) – within 10 business days;[81]
  - changes title, name or National Insurance number (using Form D) – within seven business days;[82]
  - changes arrangements (as defined in §4.3.1) (using Form D) – as soon as reasonably practicable after the firm becomes aware of the proposed change;[83]
  - revises a statement of responsibilities (using Form J);[84] or
  - has information relating to fitness, disciplinary action or a breach of COCON which needs to be disclosed (usually using Form D) – within seven business days.[85]

---

79 SUP 10C.14.1G.

80 SUP 10C.14.3G.

81 SUP 10C.14.5R, 7R. A firm must notify the FCA as soon as practicable after it becomes aware, or has information which reasonably suggests, that it will submit a qualified Form C.

82 SUP 10C.14.13R.

83 SUP 10C.14.15R.

84 FSMA s. 62A; SUP 10C.14.17G; SUP 10C.11.7D.

85 FSMA ss. 63(2A), 64C; SUP 10C.14.18R; SUP 15.11.4G. Where a general notification of a breach of COCON has already been made pursuant to SUP 15.3.11R(1)(a), and disciplinary action is subsequently taken against the person, a separate notification using Form D would still be appropriate: SUP 15.11.7G.

4.3.5 SMF Managers' Liability for Misconduct

SMF managers can be directly subject to disciplinary action by the FCA if they:

- fail to comply with the FCA's conduct rules (see §4.6.1);[86]
- are knowingly concerned in a contravention of a relevant requirement by a firm;[87] or
- were responsible for the management of an activity at a firm, in respect of which there has been a regulatory contravention, and they "*did not take such steps as a person in the [SMF] manager's position could reasonably be expected to take to avoid the contravention occurring (or continuing)*".[88] This type of personal liability is referred to by the FCA as the "**duty of responsibility**".[89]

4.4 FCA Certification Functions

4.4.1 Prior Certification by the Firm

An SMCR firm must take reasonable care to ensure that no employee performs an FCA certification function under an arrangement entered into by the firm in relation to the carrying on by the firm of a regulated activity, unless the employee has a valid certificate issued by the firm.[90]

86 FSMA s. 66A(2).

87 FSMA s. 66A(3), (4).

88 FSMA s. 66A(5).

89 SYSC 23.3.3G. Guidance on how the FCA will use its powers to take disciplinary action for breaches of the duty of responsibility is set out at DEPP 6.2.9-AG to DEPP 6.2.9-FG.

90 FSMA s. 63E(1); SYSC 27.2.3G. "**Employee**" in this context is defined in FSMA s. 63E(9).

Employees who have such a certificate are termed "**certification employees**".

In summary, "**FCA certification functions**" are defined as FCA-specified "**significant-harm functions**", which in turn are defined as functions that require the person performing it to be involved in one or more aspects of the firm's affairs, so far as relating to the activity, where those aspects involve, or might involve, a risk of significant harm to the firm or to anyone who is using, or who is or may be contemplating using, any of the services provided by the firm.[91]

The FCA certification functions are listed at SYSC 27.7.3R and defined in SYSC 27.8. A summary is set out below. Not all FCA certifications functions will be relevant to all SMCR firms.

FCA certification function	Summary
(1) CASS oversight	Acting in the capacity of a person who is allocated an oversight function in CASS 1A.3.1AR, CASS 11.3.4R or CASS 13.2.3R, as applicable. (SYSC 27.8.1R)
(2) Proprietary trader	Acting as a person whose responsibilities include committing a firm as part of its "**proprietary trading**" (defined as dealing in investments as principal as part of a business of trading in specified investments). (SYSC 27.8.3R)

91 FCA Handbook Glossary, with reference to FSMA s. 63E(2), (3), (5).

(3) Significant management	Acting as a senior manager[92] with significant responsibility for a significant business unit. (SYSC 27.8.4R)
(4) Functions requiring qualifications	Performing a function involving an activity for which there is a qualification requirement as specified in TC App 1.1.1R. (SYSC 27.8.10R)
(5) Managers of certification employees	Managing or supervising a certification employee, directly or indirectly. (SYSC 27.8.13R)
(6) Material risk takers	Each function performed by a person identified as a material risk taker (or analogous type of staff) under an applicable remuneration code (see §9.3). (SYSC 27.8.14R)
(7) Client-dealing	Carrying out a relevant activity (including advising on, dealing in, arranging or managing investments), where this involves dealing with a client or the client's property in a manner substantially connected with the carrying on of regulated activities by the firm. (SYSC 27.8.18R)

92 "**Senior manager**" is defined as including any individual (other than a director): who is employed by a firm; to whom the governing body of the firm has given responsibility for management and supervision; and who reports directly to the governing body, the chief executive or the head of a significant business unit.

(8) Algorithmic trading	Approving the deployment of a trading algorithm or an amendment to a trading algorithm or a combination of trading algorithms; or monitoring or deciding whether or not a trading algorithm is or remains compliant with the firm's obligations. (SYSC 27.8.23R)

Two notable exclusions to the obligation to issue a certificate to employees performing an FCA certification function are:

- **Emergency appointments.** A firm may appoint an employee to provide cover for a certification employee whose absence is reasonably unforeseen, for a period of less than four weeks, without such cover amounting to the performance of an FCA certification function;[93] and

- **The "30-day rule".** An employee who is based outside the UK and who spends no more than 30 days in a 12-month period in the UK (or at an overseas branch of the firm and dealing with the firm's UK clients)[94] will not be performing an FCA certification function, provided that he is appropriately supervised by one of the firm's SMF managers or a relevant certification employee.[95]

93 SYSC 27.5.1R. This exclusion does not apply to functions requiring qualifications (SYSC 27.5.1R(2), 2G).

94 Employees of a firm's (or its appointed representative's) overseas branch could in principle be within territorial scope of the FCA certification functions rules: SYSC 27.3.1R(1)(b).

95 SYSC 27.5.3R. This exclusion does not apply to functions involving: giving advice or performing related activities in connection with pension transfers, pension conversions or pension opt-outs for retail clients; (b) giving advice to a

4.4.2 SMF Managers Performing FCA Certification Functions

A function can only be an FCA certification function if it is not already a designated senior management function. Accordingly, an SMF manager performing an activity that is part of his designated senior management function does not *per se* perform an FCA certification function that comes within the description of that activity.[96]

However, if an SMF manager performs an FCA certification function that is very different from what he is doing as an SMF manager, the FCA has indicated that he must also be certified.[97] Although the FCA goes on to say that it expects this to be uncommon in larger firms in practice, it could happen for example in a financial advice firm where an SMF manager performs the SMF 3 (Executive director function), but also separately comes within the client-dealing function, and therefore needs to be both approved and certified. In this situation, firms may choose to undertake a combined fitness and propriety assessment for both the designated senior management function and the FCA certification function.

4.4.3 Procedure for Issuing Certificates

Before issuing a certificate, the firm must be satisfied that the candidate is a fit and proper person,[98] which includes the obtaining of regulatory references. Similar considerations apply as with the fitness and propriety assessment for SMF managers (see §4.3.3).

However, unlike with SMF managers, there is no specific requirement for certification employees to undergo criminal records checks. A firm

---

person to become, or continue or cease to be, a member of a particular Lloyd's syndicate; or, in the case of a UK SMCR firm, material risk takers (SYSC 27.5.3R(3), (4)).

96 FSMA s. 63E(3)(a); SYSC 27.7.5G.

97 "The Senior Managers and Certification Regime: Guide for FCA solo-regulated firms" (document, 2019).

98 FSMA s. 63F; SYSC 27.2.

may nonetheless run such a check as part of its fitness and propriety assessment, but if it does so it should note that certification employees are not included in the Rehabilitation of Offenders Act 1974 (Exceptions) Order 1975 and are therefore eligible only for a "basic" check from the Disclosure and Barring Service (as opposed to "standard" or "enhanced").

4.4.4 FCA Directory

For each certification employee, a firm must submit a duly completed and accurate report to the FCA within 7 days of commencement of the relevant FCA certification function(s).[99]

Certification employees are one type of "**Directory person**" and, as such, are included in the Financial Services Register.[100]

4.4.5 Ongoing Obligations

- **Renewal**. A certificate is valid only for a period of up to 12 months.[101] A firm must therefore refresh the certification process at least once a year. Regulatory references are unlikely to be required for such repeat assessments.[102]

- **FCA Directory**. For each certification employee, a firm must submit a duly completed and accurate report to the FCA within 7 days of any cessation of the relevant FCA certification function(s) or other change in information.[103] To the extent that no such reports have been submitted, firms must instead submit annual reports to the FCA confirming that the

---

99 SUP 16.26.6R, 13R.

100 SUP 16.26.3G(2), (3).

101 FSMA s. 63F(5); SYSC 27.2.10G.

102 "The Senior Managers and Certification Regime: Guide for FCA solo-regulated firms" (document, 2019); SYSC 22.7.5G to 8G.

103 SUP 16.26.6R, 13R.

information previously reported by the firm in respect of its Directory persons remains accurate and up-to-date.[104]

- **Record keeping.** A firm must maintain a record of every employee who has a valid certificate issued by it.[105]

4.5 Regulatory References

4.5.1 Obtaining a Regulatory Reference

When applying for a person to obtain FCA approval to perform a controlled function, or certifying an employee to perform an FCA certification function, firms must obtain regulatory references from anyone who has been the candidate's employer in the preceding six years.[106] Requests for information should be made to relevant firms in accordance with the guidance in SYSC 22.3 and 22.7.

The FCA regards this as being part of the fitness and propriety assessment and would expect to be fulfilled before the application for approval is made.[107] However, it is recognised that there may be circumstances where an application is made before regulatory references have been obtained,[108] and indeed regulatory references are formally required to be obtained only towards the end of the application process.[109]

---

104 SUP 16.26.18R.

105 FSMA s. 63F; SYSC 27.2.13G.

106 SYSC 22.2.1R.

107 "The Senior Managers and Certification Regime: Guide for FCA solo-regulated firms" (document, 2019); SYSC 22.7.11G.

108 SYSC 22.7.11G(2).

109 SYSC 22.2.3R.

A firm does not need to obtain a regulatory reference from another firm that is in the same group, to the extent that the two firms have access to the same information sources.[110]

4.5.2 Giving a Regulatory Reference

A firm that receives a request from another firm for a regulatory reference must give it to the requesting firm as soon as reasonably practicable.[111] Detailed requirements for the format of regulatory references are set out in SYSC 22.4 to 22.6.[112]

There is also a continuing obligation on firms to revise regulatory references previously given to another firm, if there is a relevant material change.[113]

4.6 Conduct Rules

4.6.1 Individual Conduct Rules and Senior Manager Conduct Rules

Although treated as an integral part of SMCR, the FCA's conduct rules for a firm's workforce, which are set out in COCON, are in fact applicable to all "**conduct rules staff**". This term encompasses not only SMF managers and certification employees, but also all other employees

---

110 SYSC 22.8A.1R(2).

111 SYSC 22.2.2R; SUP 10C.16.1G.

112 Firms may find helpful material in "Statement of Good Practice 2 – Certification Regime: Regulatory References" (Banking Standards Board, 2019).

113 SYSC 22.2.4R.

except the types of ancillary staff listed at COCON 1.1.2R row (6) column (2).[114]

All conduct rules staff must comply with the following "**individual conduct rules**" set out in COCON 2.1:[115]

Individual conduct rules	
Rule 1	You must act with integrity.
Rule 2	You must act with due skill, care and diligence.
Rule 3	You must be open and cooperative with the FCA, the PRA and other regulators.
Rule 4	You must pay due regard to the interests of customers and treat them fairly.
Rule 5	You must observe proper standards of market conduct.

SMF managers must, in addition, comply with the following "**senior manager conduct rules**" set out in COCON 2.2:[116]

114 COCON 1.1.1AR. Note that for approved persons at appointed representatives – which are not authorised firms – the Statements of Principle and Code of Practice for Approved Persons set out in APER are applicable instead of COCON (COCON 1.1.8AR). This is a remnant of the predecessor "approved persons" regime which applied to authorised firms before SMCR.

115 COCON 1.1.3R.

116 COCON 1.1.4R.

Senior manager conduct rules	
SC1	You must take reasonable steps to ensure that the business of the firm for which you are responsible is controlled effectively.
SC2	You must take reasonable steps to ensure that the business of the firm for which you are responsible complies with the relevant requirements and standards of the regulatory system.
SC3	You must take reasonable steps to ensure that any delegation of your responsibilities is to an appropriate person and that you oversee the discharge of the delegated responsibility effectively.
SC4	You must disclose appropriately any information of which the FCA or PRA would reasonably expect notice.

4.6.2 Notification of Breaches

Breaches of COCON rules must be notified to the FCA as follows:

- Significant breaches of a COCON rule, regardless of whether disciplinary action was taken, must be notified under the general notification requirement in SUP 15.3.11R(1)(a).

- Disciplinary action taken against conduct rules staff (other than SMF managers) for a breach of a COCON rule must be included in an annual return (REP008 – see §5.2.2).[117]

- Disciplinary action taken against SMF managers for a breach of a COCON rule must be notified to the FCA within seven business days – see §4.3.4.

Naturally, the notification of such breaches may in appropriate circumstances lead to enforcement action by the FCA as described in §6.

117 FSMA s. 64C(1); SUP 15.11.13R, 14R(2).

5 REGULATORY SUPERVISION

5.1 Supervisory Framework and the FCA's Approach to Supervision

Under FSMA s. 1L(1), the FCA "*must maintain arrangements for supervising authorised persons*". The FCA's overall approach to supervision is set out in SUP 1A and underpinned by the supervisory principles listed at SUP 1A.3.2AG under the following headings:

(1) *"Forward-looking";*

(2) *"A focus on strategy and business models";*

(3) *"A focus on culture and governance";*

(4) *"A focus on individual as well as firm accountability";*

(5) *"Proportionate and risk-based";*

(6) *"Two-way communication";*[118]

(7) *"Co-ordinated"; and*

(8) *"Put right systematic harm that has occurred and stop it happening again".*

---

[118] For more information on why and how the FCA communicates with firms, see "Supervisory correspondence" (webpage, 2021). The channels used by the FCA include: sending letters to senior individuals in firms; using social media platforms such as Twitter and LinkedIn; publishing the monthly "Regulation Round-up" email or "Market Watch" newsletter; proactively calling from the Contact Centre and supervisory teams; hosting industry roundtable events; senior FCA staff making speeches; and engaging with firms at public events such as the "Live and Local" programme.

The three "focuses" in the list emphasise the FCA's likely priorities when investigating or evaluating a firm, and are usefully expanded upon in "FCA Mission: Approach to Supervision" (document, 2019):

- ***Focus on strategy and business models:*** *We assess firms' strategies and business models to identify emerging risk of harm and to ensure our supervisory activity mitigates the risk they present. A strong understanding of firms' business models allows us to identify where there is poor alignment between firms' profit incentive and the interests of consumers and markets functioning well.*

- ***Focus on culture and governance:*** *We look at what drives behaviour in a firm. We address the key drivers of behaviour which are likely to cause harm. These include the firm's purpose (as it is understood by its employees), the attitude, behaviour, competence and compliance of the firm's leadership, the firm's approach to managing and rewarding people (e.g. staff competence and incentives), and the firm's governance arrangements, controls and key processes (e.g. for whistleblowing or complaint handling). When it comes to governance, we assess effectiveness, not merely design. We focus on a firm's conduct risk framework, whether the firm has effective governance arrangements in place to identify the risk of harm to consumers and markets, and whether they have a strategy in place to manage and mitigate those risks.*[119]

---

[119] Detailed insights into the FCA's thinking on culture and governance are available in the wealth of material it has issued on the topic in recent years, much of which can be accessed from "Culture and governance" (webpage, 2020).

The material includes two collections of essays in "Transforming Culture in Financial Services" (DP18/2) and "Transforming culture in financial services – Driving purposeful cultures" (DP20/1), as well as the FCA's self-reflective "Our values and core skills – A quick reference guide" (document, 2019).

In the context of supervising wholesale firms, conduct risk is the focus of the "5 Conduct Questions" programme which the FCA introduced in 2015 for banks

> ➢ ***Focus on individual as well as firm accountability:*** *We approve and hold to account the most senior individuals whose decisions and personal conduct have a significant effect on the conduct of their firm… As part of [SMCR], we also expect firms to take responsibility for certifying the competence and integrity of employees with the potential to cause significant harm.*

The FCA recognises that it relies to a degree on the co-operation of firms when gathering information for its supervisory purposes, and some of the ways in which it does so are set out in SUP 2.3. These methods are backed up, if needed, by statutory information-gathering and investigatory powers which are described in §6.1.

---

before extending it more widely across other sectors of wholesale financial markets in 2017 (see "5 Conduct Questions Programme" (webpage, 2020)). Addressing conduct risk is regarded as central to the FCA's supervisory work on wholesale firms' culture, since "*[c]ulture can be defined as the habitual mindsets and behaviours that characterise an organisation. It is at the heart of how we authorise and supervise firms, as well as where we may look for improvement*" ("'Messages from the Engine Room' – 5 Conduct Questions: Industry Feedback for 2019/20 Wholesale Banking Supervision" (document, 2020)). The eponymous questions are:

- *What proactive steps do you take as a firm to identify the conduct risks inherent within your business?*
- *How do you encourage the individuals who work in front, middle, back office, control and support functions to feel and be responsible for managing the conduct of their business?*
- *What support (broadly defined) does the firm put in place to enable those who work for it to improve the conduct of their business or function?*
- *How does the Board and ExCo (or appropriate senior management) gain oversight of the conduct of business within their organisation and, equally importantly, how does the Board or ExCo consider the conduct implications of the strategic decisions that they make?*
- *Has the firm assessed whether there are any other activities that it undertakes that could undermine strategies put in place to improve conduct?*

5.2 Periodic Reporting to the FCA

The FCA's online system for collecting and storing regulatory data from firms is called "**RegData**", and all firms are required to register for RegData as soon as possible after authorisation.

A firm's RegData schedule should reflect its integrated regulatory reporting and other periodic reporting requirements, but where any requirement has not been accurately reflected in the schedule it is incumbent upon the firm to resolve this with the FCA. An administrative fee of £250, or enforcement action, can flow from late or incomplete filings.[120]

For many of the periodic reports, template forms and guidance notes are located in the numerous annexes to SUP 16. For example, "FSA" and "FIN" reports are covered in SUP 16 Annexes 24 and 25, "CCR" reports in 38A and 38B, and MIF008 in 51 and 52. As an exception, for MIF001 to MIF007, the relevant material is in MIFIDPRU 9.

In the light of Brexit, the FCA has also issued a guide to interpreting EU-based references in FCA forms that have not yet been duly amended.[121]

5.2.1 Integrated Regulatory Reporting

A key tool used by the FCA to monitor firms' compliance with their prudential requirements is the reporting of various financial and risk-related data items within the "integrated regulatory reporting" framework detailed in SUP 16.12.[122]

The contents and frequency of data items to be submitted depend upon which one (or more) of "regulated activity group" ("**RAG**") numbers 1

120 SUP 16.3.14R, 14AG.

121 "Interpretative guide on completing our forms after the UK's withdrawal from the EU" (document, 2020).

122 For the importance attached to these prudential returns, see "Dear CEO Letter – Quality of Prudential Regulatory Returns" (document, 2018).

to 12 the firm falls within. Data items that a firm must submit under more than one RAG must only be submitted in respect of the lowest-numbered RAG.[123]

A non-SNI MIFIDPRU firm that is not a sole trader or partnership and has regulatory permissions to advise on, arrange and manage investments could fall within RAGs 3, 4 and 8, and have the following reporting schedule:

Data item	**Description**	**Frequency**
FSA029	Balance sheet	Quarterly
FSA030	Income statement	Quarterly
FSA039	Client money and client assets	Half yearly
MIF001	Capital adequacy	Quarterly
MIF002	Liquidity	Quarterly
MIF003	Metrics reporting	Quarterly
MIF004	Concentration risk (non-K-CON)	Quarterly
MIF005	Concentration risk (K-CON)	Quarterly
MIF007	ICARA assessment questionnaire	Annually

123 SUP 16.12.3R(1)(a)(ii).

A firm (not a sole trader or partnership) with regulatory permission only for managing an AIF would come within RAG 4 and, being a collective portfolio management firm within IPRU(INV) Chapter 11, would have the following reporting schedule:

Data item	Description	Frequency
FSA029	Balance sheet	Quarterly
FSA030	Income statement	Quarterly
FSA038	Volumes and type of business	Half yearly
FSA039	Client money and client assets	Half yearly
FIN066	Capital adequacy	Quarterly

Firms with permission only for credit-related regulatory activity in principle would come within RAG 12 and, if they had relevant annual revenue up to and including £5 million, would have the following reporting schedule:

Data item	Description	Frequency
CCR001	Financial data	Annually
CCR002	Volumes	Annually
CCR003	Lenders	Annually
CCR004	Debt management	Annually

CCR005	Client money and assets	Annually
CCR006	Debt collection	Annually
CCR007	Key data	Annually

5.2.2 Other Periodic Reporting

A firm can expect to have various periodic reports on their RegData schedule in addition to integrated regulatory reporting. Such additional reports may include, for investment firms:

Periodic report	**Description**	**Frequency**	**FCA Handbook ref.**
REP001	Close Links Report	Annually	SUP 16.5
REP002[124]	Controllers Report	Annually	SUP 16.4
REP008	Annual Conduct Breaches Return	Annually	SUP 15.11.13R
REP-CRIM	Annual Financial Crime Report	Annually	SUP 16.23

124 Firms should consider whether the information given in REP001 and REP002 is consistent with information about the firm's "persons with significant control" which a firm maintains or submits to Companies House pursuant to its obligations under Companies Act 2006.

Complaints DISP 1 Ann 1R	Complaints Return	Half yearly	DISP 1.10.1R; DISP 1.1A.38UK, 39R
FIN-A[125]	Annual report and accounts	Annually	SUP 16.7A
MIF008	MIFIDPRU Remuneration Report	Annually	SUP 16.29
CMAR[126]	Client Money and Assets Return	Monthly	SUP 16.14

Additionally, AIFMs that manage UK AIFs or market AIFs in the UK must submit quarterly, half-annual or annual AIFM and AIF

---

125 Firms required to file annual accounts and reports under Companies Act 2006 s. 441 should note that their deadline for submitting FIN-A to the FCA may be significantly earlier than their deadline for filing those same accounts and report with Companies House. Furthermore, under s. 475 annual accounts generally must be audited, and although there is an exemption from audit for "small companies", this exemption cannot be used by certain types of company including MiFID investment firms (s. 478).

There is also a general obligation on investment firms to establish, implement and maintain accounting policies and procedures that enable them, at the FCA's request, to deliver in a timely manner financial reports which reflect a true and fair view of their financial position and which comply with all applicable accounting standards and rules. (MiFID Org Regulation art. 21(4).)

126 Only for CASS large firms and CASS medium firms.

transparency reports to the FCA, using forms AIF001 and AIF002 respectively.[127]

All firms must check annually the accuracy of their "**firm details**" as logged in the FCA's records, which can be reviewed using the Connect online system.[128] Any changes to firm details must be communicated to the FCA.

5.3 *Ad Hoc* Notifications and Applications to the FCA

Firms must notify the FCA of any changes in the following core information:

- name, address or telephone number; or
- whether or not subject to the supervision of any overseas regulator.[129]

Other specific *ad hoc* notification and application requirements may include, as applicable:

- notifications under MIFIDPRU about a firm's prudential situation;[130]

---

127 FUND 3.4. For technical specifications, see: SUP 16.18; AIFMD Level 2 Regulation (including Annex IV); and "Guidelines on reporting obligations under Articles 3(3)(d) and 24(1), (2) and (4) of the AIFMD" (ESMA/2014/869) (ESMA, 2014).

128 SUP 16.10.

129 SUP 15.5.

130 Most notably:

- own funds or liquid assets falling below certain levels (MIFIDPRU 7.6.11R, 7.7.14R);

- changes in controllers and close links;[131]
- change of accounting reference date;[132]
- notifications and applications in relation to FCA-approved persons (including SMF managers);[133]
- notifications in relation to certification employees;[134]

- concentration risk soft limited exceeded or hard limit breached (MIFIDPRU 5.6.3R, 5.9.3R);
- issuance of additional capital instruments that have already been approved as common equity tier 1 instruments, or intended issuance of AT1 or T2 instruments, or intended reduction in own funds instruments where a condition in MIFIDPRU 3.6.4R applies (MIFIDPRU 3.3.3R(2), 3.6.5R, 3.6.3R);
- initial or revised date on which the firm will submit data item MIF007 (ICARA assessment questionnaire) (MIFIDPRU 7.8.14R);
- qualification of a non-SNI investment firm to be reclassified as an SNI investment firm, or the cessation of such qualification (MIFIDPRU 1.2.13R(2)(b), 1.2.16R);
- intended non-material change or extension to the use of an internal model (MIFIDPRU 4.12.7R);
- firm no longer satisfies all the conditions of a K-CMG permission previously granted in relation to a portfolio (MIFIDPRU 4.13.10R);
- use of an end-of-day value for CMH as a result of a qualifying error (MIFIDPRU 1.2.7R(2));
- use of the alternative approach to measure AUM and/or COH for the purpose of determining SNI status (MIFIDPRU 1.2.4R); and
- intended use of own delta estimates (MIFIDPRU 4.12.10R, 4.14.20R).

131 SUP 11. See also "Change in control" (webpage, 2021) and "Close Links" (webpage, 2016).

132 SUP 16.3.17R.

133 See 4.3.3, 4.3.4, 4.6.2.

134 See 4.4.4, 4.4.5, 4.6.2.

- changes in management body (except where the person in question performs an FCA governing function in relation to the firm in their role as a member of the management body);[135]
- intention to enter into a critical or important outsourcing arrangement;[136]
- notification under CASS to opt in to a higher category of "CASS firm type";[137]
- suspicious transactions and orders that might constitute market abuse, under MA Reg;[138]
- applications and notifications regarding obligations and exemptions under EMIR;[139] and
- errors and omissions in a firm's transaction reports.[140]

Broader event-driven notification requirements are set out in SUP 15.3, covering (most notably):

- matters having a serious regulatory impact;

---

135 SUP 15.16.4R, 6R.

136 SYSC 8.1.12G. See §8.5.2.

137 CASS 1A.2.5R.

138 MA Reg art. 16(2); SUP 15.10; "How to report suspected market abuse as a firm or trading venue" (webpage, 2021).

139 SUP 15A.1.

140 MA Reg RTS art. 15(2). These should be notified using the "Transaction reporting – Errors and omissions notification form" (document, 2018).

- matters of which the FCA would reasonably expect notice, under Principle 11;[141]
- breaches of rules and other requirements in or under FSMA or the Consumer Credit Act 1974;[142]
- civil, criminal or disciplinary proceedings against the firm;
- fraud, errors and other irregularities; and
- insolvency, bankruptcy and winding up.

For UK AIFMs, there are obligations to notify the FCA before implementing any material changes including for example:

- being appointed to manage another AIF;
- the appointment of a different depositary for an AIF the AIFM manages; and
- the appointment of any new senior personnel (unless FCA approval is required under FSMA s. 59).[143]

Notification rules often include specifications for how the notification should be made – typically, via the FCA's Connect online system, or to

---

141 These include (but are not limited to): any proposed restructuring, reorganisation or business expansion which could have a significant impact on the firm's risk profile or resources; any significant failure in the firm's systems or controls, including those reported to the firm by the firm's auditor; and any action which a firm proposes to take which would result in a material change in its capital adequacy or solvency (SUP 15.3.8G). These may also include a change of legal status, although in many such cases the FCA would require a new authorisation application to be made: see "Change of legal status" (webpage, 2021).

142 Where the breach relates to a COCON rule and leads to disciplinary action, see also §4.6.2.

143 SUP 15.3.26R to 31G.

a particular email address. Otherwise, firms should refer to the general provisions in SUP 15.7 ("Form and method of notification").

Where the notification involves a regulatory breach, this may in appropriate circumstances lead to enforcement action by the FCA as described in §6.

5.4 Annual Regulatory Fees

To fund the regulatory activities of the FCA and other bodies, firms must pay regulatory fees and levies in respect of each "**fee year**", which runs from 1 April to 31 March.

A firm receives its first regulatory invoice from the FCA in the weeks following authorisation; this first invoice is pro rata for the remaining period of the current fee year.

Thereafter, the FCA issues invoices for each fee year in July or August of that fee year. Where a firm's total fee payable exceeds £50,000, it will additionally be invoiced for an advance payment of 50% of that fee, payable around the start of the following fee year, and to be deducted in due course from that fee year's annual invoice.[144]

A regulatory invoice can be expected to comprise the following components, each of which is based on fee tariffs calculated in accordance with the following sections of the FCA Handbook:

144 FEES 4.3.6R(1C).

Component	FEES ref.
Financial Conduct Authority Periodic Fee	4.4 ("Information on which fees are calculated")
Financial Ombudsman Service Levy[145]	5.3 ("The general levy")
Financial Services Compensation Scheme Levy[146]	6.4 ("Management expenses")
Financial Guidance Levy	7A.2 ("The SFGB [single financial guidance body] levy"); 7B.2 ("The DA [Devolved Authorities] levy")

The computation of certain fee tariffs requires firms to submit specific data about the amount of business it undertakes (*e.g.*, funds under management or annual income). The FCA contacts firms each January to request such fee tariff data, and expects firms to carefully consult the relevant guidance notes[147] when preparing the return. The guidance

---

145 There is an exemption from the general levy for a firm which "*does not conduct business with eligible complainants and has no reasonable likelihood of doing so*" and has notified the FCA accordingly (FEES 5.1.4R; DISP 1.1.12R).

146 A firm can be exempt from a specific costs levy or compensation costs levy or both (but not base cost levy) if it "*does not conduct business in respect of which the Financial Services Compensation Scheme may pay compensation and has no reasonable likelihood of doing so*" and has notified the Financial Services Compensation Scheme accordingly (FEES 6.2.1AR(1)). However, a firm which is an operator, depositary, manager or trustee of a collective investment scheme should be aware of the "look-through" provision in COMP 12A.3, whereby the scheme's participants (as opposed to the scheme itself) would be treated as the claimants in a claim.

147 "Report fee tariff data" (webpage, 2021).

notes explain various technical definitions and nuances that could significantly impact a firm's calculations, which in turn can have big knock-on effects for the size of the annual fee as well as any subsequent interim or supplementary levies that could be imposed later in the fee year in response to industry-wide failings.

The FCA's Online Invoicing System can be used for submitting fee tariff data as well as paying and managing invoices.[148] Newly-authorised firms are auto-registered for the Online Invoicing System, and the FCA encourages all other firms to register as well.

5.5 Covid-19 and Remote Working: Regulatory Intervention

A practical case study of supervisory levers that can be engaged during a massively disruptive event has been provided by the ongoing Covid-19 pandemic.

Since Covid-19 was declared a pandemic by the World Health Organisation in March 2020, various regulatory interventions have been made, some originating with the FCA itself and others with ESMA (before the end of the Brexit implementation period in December 2020). These have included:[149]

- temporary modification of certain SMCR rules, including extension of the 12-week rule (see §4.3.1) to up to 36 weeks through a modification by consent, and relief from notifying the FCA of changes in arrangements or updated statements of responsibilities (see §4.3.4);
- temporary waiver of administrative fees for late returns of certain regulatory filings including FIN-A and certain fund

148 Amounts invoiced can be checked using the FCA's interactive "Fee calculator" (webpage, 2021).

149 "Coronavirus (Covid-19): Information for firms" (webpage, 2021).

reports and accounts, representing an extension of (typically) one or two months;

- Covid-19 impact surveys required to be completed by sampled firms, focusing on financial resilience and mandatory under FSMA s. 165 (see §6.1);

- temporary relief on the requirement for firms to issue 10% depreciation notifications to investors (see §11.4.2);

- lowering of threshold for notifying net short positions in response to volatility in the financial markets (see §13.1.2);

- recognition that in some exceptional circumstances it may not be practicable to comply with the rules requiring certain telephone conversations to be recorded (see §8.6.2), and that it may be appropriate for a firm which cannot so comply to take alternative steps instead to mitigate the risks related to the lack of recording;[150]

- publishing webpages emphasising regulatory expectations and firms' existing responsibilities in relation to operational resilience, information security, securities trading and reporting, and financial crime systems and controls;

- publishing detailed guidance on regulatory expectations for treating customers fairly during the pandemic, especially in the context of insurance and consumer finance businesses;[151] and

- confirmation that firms may use electronic signatures for all interactions with the FCA.

---

150 "Public Statement – COVID-19: Clarification of issues related to the application of MiFID II requirements on the recording of telephone conversations" (ESMA35-43-2348) (ESMA, 2020).

151 "Published coronavirus (Covid-19) guidance for firms" (webpage, 2021).

One important practical corollary of the pandemic has been a significant shift in firms' operations towards remote or hybrid arrangements. The FCA considers it "*likely many firms will continue these new ways of working*", and to address this has published a statement which details its regulatory expectations regarding:

- what existing firms should plan for, in terms of how firms operate their business, firms' engagement with the FCA, and notifying the FCA of changes to a firm's working arrangements; and

- firms that are applying to be authorised or registered.[152]

The statement notes that the FCA's "*expectations will evolve as more is understood about how firms intend to operate*", but does nevertheless make clear that firms proposing to dispense with a centralised location or implement a significant degree of remote working need to be in a position to prove that such arrangements will not, or are unlikely to, affect their compliance with the regulatory system or the FCA's ability to exercise its supervisory powers effectively.

---

152 "Remote or hybrid working expectations for firms" (webpage, 2021).

6 ENFORCEMENT

The FCA has a wide range of statutory enforcement powers – which is to say, powers to investigate regulatory contraventions and take regulatory, criminal or civil action.

Many of those powers are contained in FSMA, which also requires the FCA to prepare and publish statements of policy or procedure governing the exercise of those powers. Those statements are published in DEPP.[153]

Further high-level information about the FCA's approach to enforcement is contained in its Enforcement Guide ("**EG**")[154] as well as more concise overviews including "Enforcement Information Guide" (document, 2017) and "FCA Mission: Approach to Enforcement" (document, 2019).

FCA enforcement outcomes are summarised and published in its "Enforcement data – Annual Reports" (webpages, various). Data from the three most recent reports to 2020/21 show that 652 enforcement cases were closed during that period. The average length of all regulatory and civil enforcement cases was just under two years, and the most common outcome (at almost 80% of the total) was variation, cancellation or withdrawal of approval/permission. Financial penalties were imposed in relatively few cases (about 6% of the total), but amounted to a substantial sum of £641.5m.

---

153 For lists of specific statutory requirements and powers in relation to the publication of such statements, see DEPP 1.1.2G and Schedule 4.

154 EG 1.1.8 clarifies that "*the material in this guide does not form part of the FCA Handbook and is not guidance on rules, but it is 'general guidance' as defined in section 139B of the Act*". This contrasts with "guidance" made under s. 139A FSMA, compliance with which is formally treated by the FCA as compliance with the rule or requirement to which that guidance relates ("Reader's Guide: An introduction to the Handbook" (document, 2021)).

In terms of subject matter, as at 31 March 2021 the FCA had 794 open cases which largely comprised threshold conditions/fitness and propriety (25%), unauthorised business (22%), retail conduct (13%) and insider dealing (9%).

Other, non-FCA enforcement regimes also exist which may be relevant to firms – for example, those of the ICO, Advertising Standards Agency, local authorities, Competition and Markets Authority, Serious Fraud Office or the police. Those enforcement regimes are out of scope of this book.

6.1 Investigations

The FCA's main information-gathering and investigatory powers are contained in Part XI of FSMA. Failure to comply with a requirement imposed under that Part can amount to a criminal offence under s. 177.

Factors which drive the FCA's decision to open an investigation are set out in EG 2, which refers also to "Investigation opening criteria" (webpage, 2019).

Under FSMA s. 165, the FCA may by written notice require an authorised person to provide information or documents. Further, a report on the matter concerned – provided by either the person concerned or a qualified appointee (a "**skilled person**") – may be required under s. 166. For guidance, see EG 3.

Where the FCA wishes to proceed with an investigation, investigators may be appointed under FSMA ss. 167 (general investigations) or 168 (specified circumstances). The conduct of FCA investigations is governed by ss. 170 to 176A, including: the requirement for notices (s. 170(2)); the admissibility of statements made to investigators (s. 174); powers to require information and documents from third parties (s. 175(1)); and entry of premises under warrant (s. 176). For guidance, see EG 4.

In relation to more specific areas, certain additional information-gathering and investigatory powers are contained in FSMA ss. 97 (official list), 122A to 122C (market abuse), 131E to 131FC (short selling) and 284 (collective investment schemes). The FCA also has powers to assist overseas regulators under ss. 169 (general) and 131FA (short selling) of FSMA.[155]

A survey of the FCA's analogous powers under a wide range of non FSMA statutory provisions is set out in EG 19 and 20.

The FCA's conduct of investigations is subject two important general restrictions:

- Under FSMA s.348, the FCA usually may not disclose "**confidential information**", which covers information relating to the business or other affairs of any person which has not legitimately been made public and can be ascertained as information relating to a particular person.

- Under FSMA s.413, a person may not be required to produce, disclose or permit the inspection of "**protected items**", which covers relevant communications made in connection with either the giving of professional legal advice or legal proceedings.[156] However, firms should note that, if they do provide such information to the FCA, there is a risk that such protection may be waived in its entirety and that the FCA "*cannot 'close its eyes' to information received or accept*

---

155 Where an FCA investigation may involve an interview that is attended by a representative of an overseas regulator, the "statement of policy on interviews conducted on behalf of overseas regulators" published at DEPP 7 could be engaged.

156 This restriction is similar to a person's common law rights to legal professional privilege which, if properly engaged, protect confidential communications between the person and its lawyers from disclosure to third parties in case of civil action, under the sub-doctrines of legal advice privilege or litigation privilege. A recent landmark decision which considers the scope of legal professional privilege (especially litigation privilege) in the context of regulatory and criminal investigations is *Director of the Serious Fraud Office v Eurasian Natural Resources Corporation Limited* [2018] EWCA Civ 2006.

that information should, say, be used only for the purposes of supervision but not for enforcement".[157]

6.2 Decisions and Penalties

The first direct outcome of the investigation process will be a decision by the FCA as to whether or not action should be taken. In making this decision, the FCA should have regard to factors set out in the applicable provisions of EG and DEPP as referred to in the table below.

Where the FCA considers it appropriate, it may decide to close the investigation at any stage in the procedure without taking any further action.[158]

Alternatively, should the FCA decide that action may be appropriate, its statutory enforcement powers will be engaged. Powers in relation to firms and their staff include, most notably:

Power	**FSMA ref.**	**FCA Handbook ref.**
REGULATORY POWERS		
Vary or cancel firm's Part 4A permission.	s.55J	EG 8
Imposition of requirements on firm.	s.55L	EG 8
Prohibition order on person for lack of fitness and propriety.	s.56	EG 9

157 EG 3.11.13.

158 "Enforcement Information Guide" (document, 2017).

Withdrawal of person's approval for lack of fitness and propriety.	s.63	EG 9
Financial penalty on person performing a controlled function without approval.[159]	s.63A	EG 7; DEPP 6
Vary SMF manager's approval on FCA's own initiative.	s.63ZB	DEPP 8
Action against approved persons and conduct rules staff: • Financial penalty; • Suspension of approval; • Conditions in relation to approval; • Limitation of period for which approval is to have effect; • Publication of statement of misconduct.	s.66	EG 7; DEPP 6, 6A
Financial penalty, public censure and certain other prohibitions in connection with market abuse.	ss.123 to 123B	EG 7; DEPP 6
Financial penalty and public censure in connection with short selling.	s.131G	EG 7; DEPP 6

159 So that the purpose of financial penalties is not frustrated, as a general rule firms are not allowed to pay financial penalties imposed on their staff and are also prohibited from obtaining insurance against financial penalties (GEN 6.1.4AR, 5R).

Public censure against firm.	s.205	EG 7; DEPP 6
Financial penalty on firm.	s.206	EG 7; DEPP 6
Suspension or limitation of period of regulatory permission in relation to firm.	s.206A	EG 7; DEPP 6A
Require restitution.	s.384	EG 11
CIVIL POWERS		
Apply to court for administration order.	s.359	EG 13
Petition court for winding-up order.	s.367	EG 13
Apply to court for injunction of breach of relevant requirement, including asset-freezing injunctions.	s.380	EG 10
Apply to court for injunction in case of market abuse, including asset-freezing injunctions.	s.381	EG 10
Apply to court for restitution order for breach of relevant requirement.	s.382	EG 11
Apply to court for restitution order in case of market abuse.	s.383	EG 11

CRIMINAL POWERS		
Prosecution for offences under FSMA and Financial Services Act 2012 Part 7.	s.401	EG 12
Prosecution for offences in relation to insider dealing, money laundering and terrorist financing.	s.402	EG 12

In cases where regulatory action is being considered, the FCA can be expected to proceed broadly along the following lines:

- **Preliminary findings**. The FCA sends a preliminary findings letter to the person concerned, annexing the investigators' preliminary investigation report. The person concerned is invited to comment within 28 days.[160]

- **If the person concerned agrees all relevant issues**, two members of the FCA's senior management are appointed to act as "**settlement decision makers**" and decide whether to accept or decline the proposed settlement.[161] If the decision is to accept the proposed settlement and a settlement agreement is duly entered into with the person concerned, the settlement decision makers issue the relevant "**statutory notices**", which comprise "**warning notices**" (FSMA s.387), "**decision notices**" (s.388) and "**supervisory notices**" (s.395).[162] If the decision is to decline the

[160] EG 4.13.

[161] EG 5.3; DEPP 5.1.1G to 8G.

[162] Descriptions of each type of statutory notice are set out in DEPP 2. Essentially: warning notices are issued where the FCA proposes to take certain action; decision notices are issued where, after considering any representations made on a warning notice, the FCA decides to take action; and supervisory notices are issued

proposed settlement, further discussions may be held, or the settlement decision makers may escalate the matter to the FCA's "**Regulatory Decisions Committee**".[163]

- **If the person concerned wishes to partly contest the proposed action**, discussions may then be held with a view to entering into a "**focused resolution agreement**".[164] The settlement decision makers may at their discretion decline to enter into such an agreement, in which case further discussions may be held (or by default the procedures for statutory notices would be followed in the usual way).

- **If the person concerned wishes to challenge the proposed action without engaging with the FCA's internal decision-making process**, it may do so by using the "**expedited reference procedure**" in order to refer the matter directly to the Upper Tribunal (Tax and Chancery Chamber) ("**Tribunal**").[165] An overview of the Tribunal is given in §6.3.

The FCA operates a "**settlement discount scheme**" which is designed to encourage the timely settlement of cases by offering a reduction in the financial penalty or duration of suspension, restriction or condition that

---

where the FCA decides that a variation of permission and/or requirement(s) should be imposed on a firm. The FCA's procedure for making statutory notice decisions under executive procedures (*i.e.*, not involving escalation to the Regulatory Decisions Committee) is described at DEPP 4.1.

163 For the general ability of FCA staff to make a recommendation to the Regulatory Decisions Committee that a warning notice should be given, see DEPP 3.2.12G. The Regulatory Decisions Committee is an organ of the FCA board that operates separately from the rest of the FCA. Its process is administrative, not judicial, in that it is the final stage of decision-making within the FCA as opposed to an appeal body. For more information, see DEPP 3 and "Regulatory Decisions Committee (RDC)" (webpage, 2021).

164 EG 5.3; DEPP 5.1.8AG to 8DG.

165 DEPP 5.1.8EG to 8JG.

would otherwise be imposed, depending upon the stage at which a settlement agreement is reached.[166]

Mediation may be used in appropriate cases,[167] although the FCA acknowledges that mediation has only a limited role in regulating financial services and will usually only be appropriate in cases where settlement may not otherwise be satisfactorily achieved.[168]

6.3 References to the Tribunal

A firm may refer an enforcement matter to the Tribunal where: it disagrees with a decision notice;[169] or pursuant to the expedited reference procedure described in §6.2; or under any of the various provisions in FSMA which apply to other specific types of FCA decision.

The Tribunal is part of the Upper Tribunal, a superior court of record established by the Tribunals, Courts and Enforcement Act 2007 s. 3 and, as such, independent of the FCA.

In terms of procedure, the Tribunal may consider any evidence whether or not available at the time of the decision notice (*i.e.*, it considers cases afresh), and in FCA disciplinary reference cases it will determine what (if any) action it is appropriate for the FCA to take and then remit the matter to the FCA with appropriate directions.[170]

---

166 EG 5.5; DEPP 6.7.

167 EG 5.6; DEPP 5.1.9G.

168 "Settlement and mediation in enforcement cases" (webpage, 2021).

169 FSMA s. 127(4).

170 FSMA s.133. More granular details about the Tribunal's procedure in financial services cases are contained in The Tribunal Procedure (Upper Tribunal) Rules 2008, s. 26B and Schedule 3.

Appeals from the Tribunal – on points of law only – lie to the Court of Appeal in England and Wales (or equivalent courts in Scotland or Northern Ireland), or directly to the Supreme Court.[171]

Note that the existence of a statutory appeal procedure of this kind ordinarily precludes an application to the High Court for judicial review of the regulator's original decision, save in exceptional circumstances.[172]

6.4 Conclusion of Proceedings

If the FCA terminates an investigation or subsequent enforcement action prior to the issuing of a warning notice, there is no statutory obligation to notify the person concerned. However, if formal notice of appointment of an investigator has already been served by the time the termination decision is made, the FCA will usually give confirmation of the decision.[173]

If the decision to discontinue proceedings is made after a warning notice or decision notice has been given, the FCA must usually give a notice of discontinuance under FSMA s. 389.

Alternatively, if proceedings continue to their conclusion and the FCA takes action as has been set out in a decision notice, a "**final notice**" must be issued under FSMA s. 390.

6.5 Publication

At the investigation stage before any statutory notices have been issued, the FCA will not make any information public other than in exceptional circumstances.[174]

---

171 Tribunals, Courts and Enforcement Act 2007 ss. 13 to 14C.

172 *R (Willford) v Financial Services Authority* [2013] EWCA Civ 677.

173 EG 4.5.1.

174 EG 6.1.

For decision notices, final notices and supervisory notices, the FCA generally must publish such information as it considers appropriate, but only if publication would not be unfair to the person concerned, prejudicial to the interests of consumers or detrimental to the stability of the UK financial system. For disciplinary warning notices, the situation is similar except that such publication is permitted (not mandatory), and the FCA must additionally first consult the person concerned before it can publish.[175] To view published notices and decisions, see "Publications" (webpage, various).

Before the Tribunal, hearings must generally be held in public unless the Tribunal gives a direction that a hearing (or part of it) is to be held in private.[176]

Records of the Tribunal (as with all courts of record) are formally designated "public records" coming within the ambit of the Keeper of Public Records and the Lord Chancellor;[177] in practice this means that Tribunal judgments are often made available to the public in multiple locations, including via the Public Record Office (merged into the National Archives in 2003) and the websites of the UK Government and the British and Irish Legal Information Institute. From April 2022 Tribunal judgments are due to start being published online in a more standardised way by the National Archives.[178]

---

175 FSMA s. 391(1), (4), (5), (6); DEPP 5.1.8KG to 8QG; EG 6.2. Additional provisions about publication which apply in specific circumstances are set out in FSMA ss. 391A to 391F and EG 6.4 to 10.

176 The Tribunal Procedure (Upper Tribunal) Rules 2008, s. 37.

177 Public Records Act 1958 ss. 2(3), 8(1) and Schedule 4(1)(b).

178 "Boost for open justice as court judgments get new home" (UK Government webpage, 2021).

PART B

SYSTEMS & CONTROLS

7 GOVERNANCE AND STAFF ORGANISATIONAL REQUIREMENTS

A multi-layered regulatory framework exists that seeks to positively influence the conduct of management and staff at all levels within a firm, and aims to ensure that a satisfactory calibre of staff is hired in the first place.

Considered below are:

- specifications for the composition and responsibilities of a firm's management body, as set out in SYSC, MiFID Org Regulation and MIFIDPRU; and

- the organisational requirements in MiFID Org Regulation which are concerned with the competence of a firm's workforce, the control of certain types of personal conflicts of interest, and whistleblowing.

Other important components of the regulatory framework for governance and conduct, which are dealt with elsewhere in this book, include:

- the SMCR rules applicable to SMF managers and staff performing FCA Certification Functions (see §4.3 to §4.6);

- remuneration codes (including the MIFIDPRU Remuneration Code) covering a firm's material risk takers (see §9.3); and

- applicable conduct rules in COCON with which all non-ancillary staff must comply (see §4.6).

7.1 Governance

SYSC 4.3A concerns a firm's "**management body**", which is defined as (in summary) the governing body[179] and senior personnel[180] who are empowered to set the firm's strategy, objectives and overall direction, and which oversee and monitor management decision-making.

7.1.1 Composition of Management Body

When constituting the management body, firms must ensure that:

- members of the management body do not hold more directorships than is appropriate taking into account individual circumstances and the nature, scale and complexity of the firm's activities;[181]
- the management body comprises at least two persons;[182]
- adequate human and financial resources are devoted to the induction and training of members of the management body;[183] and
- a broad set of qualities and competences is engaged when recruiting members to the management body and, for that

---

179 "**Governing body**" is defined as (essentially) "*the board of directors, committee of management or other governing body of a firm*".

180 "**Senior personnel**" is defined as (essentially) "*those persons who effectively direct the business of the firm... which could include the membership of the governing body and other individuals who effectively direct the business of the person*".

181 SYSC 4.3A.5R.

182 SYSC 4.2.2R.

183 SYSC 4.3A.4R.

purpose, a policy promoting diversity on the management body is put in place.[184]

The minimum qualifications for members of the management body are listed at SYSC 4.3A.3R,[185] and (as referred to at SYSC 4.3A.3AG) guidelines on assessing their suitability have been jointly issued by ESMA and the EBA.[186]

Firms should remember that changes in composition of the management body may require approval from, or notification to, the FCA if the staff in question is an SMF manager (see §4.3.4) or is a member of the management body who is not performing an FCA governing function (§5.3).

7.1.2 Responsibilities of Management Body

The management body is responsible for defining, overseeing and being accountable for "*the implementation of governance arrangements that ensure effective and prudent management of a firm, including the segregation of duties and the prevention of conflicts of interest, and in a manner that promotes the integrity of the market and the interests of clients*". These and other specifications are set out at SYSC 4.3A.1R and 1AR.

---

184 SYSC 4.3A.10R.

185 Namely, they must: be of sufficiently good repute; possess sufficient knowledge, skills and experience to perform their duties; possess adequate collective knowledge, skills and experience to understand the firm's activities, including the main risks; reflect an adequately broad range of experiences; commit sufficient time to perform their functions in the firm; and act with honesty, integrity and independence of mind to effectively assess and challenge the decisions of senior management where necessary and to effectively oversee and monitor management decision-making.

186 "Final report – Joint ESMA and EBA Guidelines – on the assessment of the suitability of members of the management body and key function holders under Directive 2013/36/EU and Directive 2014/65/EU" (EBA/GL/2017/12) (ESMA and EBA, 2017).

For investment firms, such "**governance arrangements**" include the following elements of MiFID Org Regulation art. 21(1):

- decision-making procedures and an organisational structure which clearly and in documented manner specifies reporting lines and allocates functions and responsibilities;[187]

- adequate internal control mechanisms designed to secure compliance with decisions and procedures at all levels of the investment firm; and

- effective internal reporting and communication of information at all relevant levels of the investment firm.

As a general matter, all such arrangements, processes and mechanisms must be comprehensive and proportionate to the nature, scale and complexity of (1) the risks inherent in the business model and (2) the firm's activities.[188]

Further, under MiFID Org Regulation art. 25, a firm must ensure that senior management:[189]

- are responsible for ensuring that the firm complies with UK law on markets in financial instruments, including being required to assess and periodically review the effectiveness of the policies, arrangements and procedures put in place to comply with those obligations and to take appropriate measures to address any deficiencies; and

---

187 See also SYSC 4.1.1R(1).

188 MiFID Org Regulation art. 21(1); SYSC 4.1.2R.

189 "**Senior management**" is defined as "*those persons who are a natural person, who exercise executive functions in common platform firms and who are responsible and accountable to the management body for the day-to-day management of the firm, including for the implementation of the policies concerning the distribution of services and products to clients by it and its personnel*".

- receive, at least annually, written reports on compliance, risk management and internal audit matters indicating in particular whether the appropriate remedial measures have been taken in the event of any deficiencies.

7.1.3 MIFIDPRU Governance and Risk Management Provisions

MIFIDPRU investment firms are subject to supplemental provisions in MIFIDPRU 7.2 which mandate robust governance arrangements and require that the management body of a MIFIDPRU investment firm has overall responsibility for risk management.[190]

Further, under MIFIDPRU 7.3 non-SNI MIFIDPRU investment firms which exceed prescribed quantitative ceilings[191] must establish risk, remuneration and nomination committees.

7.2 Staff Organisational Requirements

7.2.1 Skills, Knowledge and Expertise of Staff

Under MiFID Org Regulation art. 21(1)(d), firms must "*employ personnel with the skills, knowledge and expertise necessary for the discharge*

---

190 MIFIDPRU 7.2.1R, 7.2.3R. For MIFIDPRU provisions on the risk management function, see §10.3.2.

191 The following quantitative ceilings are prescribed by MIFIDPRU 7.1.4R(1): (a) where the value of the firm's on-balance sheet assets and off-balance sheet items over the preceding 4-year period is a rolling average of £100 million or less; or (b) where: (i) the value of the firm's on-balance sheet assets and off-balance sheet items over the preceding 4-year period is a rolling average of £300 million or less; and (ii) the conditions in (2) are (where they are relevant to a firm) satisfied. The conditions in (2) are: (a) that the exposure value of the firm's on- and off-balance sheet trading book business is equal to or less than £150 million; and (b) that the exposure value of the firm's on- and off-balance sheet derivatives business is equal to or less than £100 million.

of the responsibilities allocated to them". FCA guidance on assessing skills, knowledge and expertise is set out in SYSC 5.1.2G to 5AG.

On an ongoing basis, firms must ensure that relevant persons are aware of the procedures which must be followed for the proper discharge of their responsibilities.[192]

Firms must, in particular, be able to demonstrate to the FCA, at the FCA's request, that any relevant individuals possess the necessary knowledge and competence so as to ensure that the firm is able to meet its obligations under the MiFID investor protection rules relating to information to clients, assessment of suitability and appropriateness, and reporting to clients (as located in COBS and PROD).[193] As noted in SYSC 5.1.5ADG, ESMA has issued guidelines on assessing knowledge and competence for these purposes.[194]

Where a firm's business involves certain advisory, dealing and other services for retail clients (and other similar types of customer) as defined in TC App 1.1, the firm must comply with additional, more prescriptive competence and record-keeping requirements in TC 2 and 3 respectively in relation to those of its employees who carry out those activities.

---

192 MiFID Org Regulation art. 21(1)(b). See also "Training and competence" (webpage, 2021).

"**Relevant person**" is defined as: "*(a) a director, partner or equivalent, manager or tied agent of the firm; (b) a director, partner or equivalent, or manager of any tied agent of the firm; (c) an employee of the firm or of a tied agent of the firm, as well as any other natural person whose services are placed at the disposal and under the control of the firm or a tied agent of the firm and who is involved in the provision by the firm of investment services and activities; (d) a natural person who is directly involved in the provision of services to the investment firm or to its tied agent under an outsourcing arrangement for the purpose of the provision by the firm of investment services and activities*" (MiFID Org Regulation art. 2(1)).

193 SYSC 5.1.5ABR to 5BR.

194 "Guidelines for the assessment of knowledge and competence" (ESMA71-1154262120-153) (ESMA, 2017).

7.2.2 MiFID Remuneration Incentives

MiFID Org Regulation art. 27 requires investment firms to define and implement remuneration policies and practices that apply to all staff who have an impact on the firm's services or corporate behaviour and whose remuneration may create a conflict of interest with the firm's clients. Equivalent requirements apply to MiFID optional exemption firms.[195]

Investment firms (including MiFID optional exemption firms) are explicitly forbidden under SYSC 19F.1.3R from:

- remunerating or assessing the performance of their staff in a way that conflicts with the firm's duty to act in the best interests of its clients; or
- making any arrangement by way of remuneration, sales targets or otherwise that could provide an incentive to their staff to recommend a particular financial instrument to a retail client when the firm could offer a different financial instrument which would better meet that client's needs.

ESMA has published guidelines on remuneration policies and practices under MiFID I, which the FCA has indicated remain relevant under MiFID II.[196]

Note that MIFID remuneration incentive provisions are supplemental to any applicable remuneration codes (including the MIFIDPRU Remuneration Code), as described in §9.3.

---

[195] SYSC 19F.1.4R.

[196] "Guidelines – Remuneration policies and practices (MiFID)" (ESMA/2013/606) (ESMA, 2013); "Remuneration and performance management of sales staff (SYSC 19F)" (webpage, 2021).

7.2.3 Segregation of Functions

Under SYSC 5.1.7R, a firm's senior personnel "*must define arrangements concerning the segregation of duties within the firm and the prevention of conflicts of interest*".

One aspect of this is detailed in MiFID Org Regulation art. 21(1)(g), whereby a firm must ensure that the performance of multiple functions by its relevant persons does not and is not likely to prevent those persons from discharging any particular function soundly, honestly, and professionally.

FCA guidance recommends that no single individual should normally have unrestricted authority to do all of the following:

- initiate a transaction;
- bind the firm;
- make payments; and
- account for it.[197]

Further, where a firm is unable to ensure the complete segregation of duties (for example, because it has a limited number of staff), it should ensure that there are adequate compensating controls in place (for example, frequent review of an area by relevant senior managers).[198]

7.2.4 Personal Account Dealing

A "**personal transaction**" is defined as "*a trade in a financial instrument effected by or on behalf of a relevant person*", where "*the relevant person is acting outside the scope of the activities he carries out in his professional capacity*" and/or "*the trade is carried out for the account of... (i) the relevant*

---

197 SYSC 5.1.9G.

198 SYSC 5.1.10G.

person; (ii) any person with whom he has a family relationship,[199] *or with whom he has close links; [or] (iii) a person in respect of whom the relevant person has a direct or indirect material interest in the outcome of the trade, other than obtaining a fee or commission for the execution of the trade*".[200]

Where a relevant person's role involves (essentially) (i) activities that may give rise to a conflict of interest or (ii) access to inside information or other confidential information relating to clients or client transactions, firms must ensure that the relevant person does not:

- enter into personal transactions that are prohibited under MA Reg, or that involve the misuse or improper disclosure of such confidential information, or conflict or are likely to conflict with an obligation of the firm under UK law on markets in financial instruments;

- improperly advise or recommend any other person to enter into a transaction which, if it were a personal transaction of the relevant person, would be prohibited under the MiFID Org Regulation; or

- improperly disclose any information or opinion to any other person

- where such relevant person knows, or reasonably ought to know, that as a result of that disclosure that other person will or would be likely to enter into such a transaction or advise or procure another person to enter into such a transaction.[201]

---

199 "**Family relationship**" includes (essentially): a spouse or partner considered by national law as equivalent to a spouse; a dependent child or stepchild; and any other relative who has shared the same household as the relevant person for at least one year on the date of the personal transaction concerned (MiFID Org Regulation art. 2(1)).

200 MiFID Org Regulation art. 28 (= COBS 11.7A.4UK).

201 MiFID Org Regulation art. 29(1)-(4) (= COBS 11.7A.5UK).

Firms must have arrangements designed to ensure that:

- relevant persons are aware of the restrictions on personal transactions, and of the measures established by the firm in connection with personal transactions and disclosure;
- the firm is informed promptly of any personal transaction entered into by relevant persons, either by notification or other procedures; and
- a record is kept of the personal transaction notified to the firm or identified by the firm, including any authorisation or prohibition in connection with such a transaction.[202]

7.2.5 Whistleblowing

MiFID investment firms are subject to the whistleblowing obligations at SYSC 18.6.1R and may also (depending on the nature of their business) have to comply with other similar whistleblowing regimes such as those listed at SYSC 18.6.4G. Generally, the obligations on a firm are to have appropriate procedures in place for its employees to report potential or actual breaches internally.

Separate whistleblowing obligations are set out in SYSC 18.3 to 18.5, which in principle apply only to banks.[203] However, FCA guidance suggests that MiFID investment firms may wish to take into consideration the list of whistleblowing arrangements in SYSC 18.3.1R(2) when formalising their own procedures.[204]

---

202 MiFID Org Regulation art. 29(5) (= COBS 11.7A.5UK).

203 SYSC 18.1.1AAG.

204 SYSC 18.6.3G.

The FCA and PRA have previously given consideration to the question of whether to introduce financial incentives for whistleblowers, and decided against doing so.[205]

[205] "Financial Incentives for Whistleblowers – Note by the Financial Conduct Authority and the Prudential Regulation Authority for the Treasury Select Committee" (FCA and PRA, 2014).

8 OPERATIONAL INFRASTRUCTURE

8.1 Data Control

Memorably likened by the Court of Appeal to an ice cube ("*give it to the party who has no refrigerator or will not agree to keep it in one, and... you have just a pool of water which neither party wants*"),[206] confidential information is recognised by lawmakers and the FCA to be a uniquely brittle asset.

Under SYSC 4.1.1R(3) a firm "*must have sound security mechanisms in place for the following, while maintaining the confidentiality of the data at all times: (a) to guarantee the security and authentication of the means of transfer of information; (b) to minimise the risk of data corruption and unauthorised access; and (c) to prevent information leakage*".[207]

The FCA repeatedly draws firms' attention to the increasing number, scale and sophistication of cyberattacks which can leave sensitive information exposed, and publishes infographics, statements, review findings and other guidance on its website.[208] Data security is also covered in FCG 5 (see §10.2.3).

8.1.1 Personal Data

UK general data protection legislation governs the processing or control of "**personal data**", which is defined as:

> *any information relating to an identified or identifiable natural person ('data subject'); an identifiable natural person is one who can*

---

206 *Attorney-General v Newspapers Publishing Plc.* [1987] EWCA Civ J0717-2.

207 MiFID Org Regulation art. 21(2) has a less granular version of this requirement.

208 See "Operational resilience" (webpage, 2021).

> *be identified, directly or indirectly, in particular by reference to an identifier such as a name, an identification number, location data, an online identifier or to one or more factors specific to the physical, physiological, genetic, mental, economic, cultural or social identity of that natural person.*[209]

"**Processing**" includes most forms of handling, such as collecting, using, storing, retrieving, disclosing or erasing,[210] while a firm is a "**controller**" of personal data where it "*alone or jointly with others, determines the purposes and means of the processing of personal data*".[211]

The FCA regards the lawful processing and transfer of client data as relevant to Principles 3 ("Management and control"), 6 ("Customers' interests") and 7 ("Communications with clients").[212] There is also a formal Memorandum of Understanding between the FCA and the main supervisory authority for data protection, the ICO, which covers cooperation, coordination and information-sharing between the bodies.[213]

At a high level, the following sets of rules under GDPR apply to data processors and controllers alike:

---

209 GDPR art. 4(1).

210 GDPR art. 4(2).

211 GDPR art. 4(7).

212 "FCA warns firms to be responsible when handling client data" (webpage, 2020).

213 "Memorandum of Understanding between the Information Commissioner and the Financial Conduct Authority" (ICO and FCA, 2019).

Set of rules	**Legislative ref.**
Data protection principles, namely: lawfulness, fairness and transparency; purpose limitation; data minimization; accuracy; storage limitation; and integrity and confidentiality. "**Lawfulness, fairness and transparency**" includes the requirement to have a lawful basis for processing, namely: consent; contract; legal obligation; vital interests; public task; or legitimate interest.[214] "Special category" and "criminal offences" data must, additionally, be processed in accordance with GDPR arts. 9 or 10 respectively.[215]	GDPR art. 5(1)
Data subjects' rights, namely: to be informed; of access; to rectification; to erasure; to restrict processing; to data portability; to object; and in relation to automated decision-making (including profiling).[216] The "right to be informed" includes a proactive obligation to provide all data subjects with "privacy information" as prescribed in GDPR arts. 13 and 14.	GDPR arts. 12 to 22
Written contracts with data processors or sub-processors.	GDPR art. 28(3)

214 GDPR art. 6(1).

215 Supplemental conditions and limitations for processing "special category" and "criminal offences" data (provided for under GDPR arts. 9 and 10) are located in the Data Protection Act 2018 ss. 10 and 11 and Schedule 1.

216 Subject to certain exemptions (created under GDPR art. 23) in the Data Protection Act 2018, Schedule 2.

Records of processing activities.	GDPR art. 30
Restriction on data transfers outside the UK, except on the basis of an adequacy decision or "appropriate safeguards".[217]	GDPR arts. 44 to 46
Appointment of "data protection officer" where (most notably) the processing requires "regular and systematic monitoring of data subjects on a large scale" or involves "processing on a large scale of" "special category" or "criminal offences" data.	GDPR arts. 37 to 39

The following sets of additional rules apply to data controllers:[218]

Set of rules	**Legislative ref.**
"Accountability" – that is, being responsible for, and being able to demonstrate compliance with, the data protection principles. Related to this is the requirement in GDPR art. 24 to implement appropriate technical and organisational measures to ensure and be able to demonstrate that processing is performance in accordance with GDPR.	GDPR art. 5(2)

217 Important derogations from the general restriction on such transfers are available in art. 49. These include where "*the transfer is necessary for important reasons of public interest*" (art. 49(1)(d)), which is the subject of a published ICO comfort letter to the U.S. Securities and Exchange Commission (James Dipple-Johnstone to Raquel Fox, 11 September 2020).

218 Relevant guidance and tools to assist with compliance (such as checklists and contract builders) are published on the ICO website.

Data protection by design and by default.	GDPR art. 25
Personal data breaches: requirement to notify supervisory authority within 72 hours, unless the breach is unlikely to result in a risk to the rights and freedoms of natural persons.	GDPR art. 33
Personal data breaches: requirement to communicate to data subjects[219] without undue delay, unless the breach is unlikely to result in a risk to the rights and freedoms of natural persons or any of the operational conditions in GDPR art. 34(3) are met.	GDPR art. 34
Conduct a data protection impact assessment, where processing is likely to result in a high risk to the rights and freedoms of natural persons and (where the inherent risk is assessed as high) consult with the supervisory authority.[220]	GDPR arts. 35, 36
Pay the ICO an annual data protection fee and be entered into the data protection register.	Data Protection (Charges and Information) Regulations 2018

219 Subject to certain exemptions (created under GDPR art. 23) in the Data Protection Act 2018, Schedule 2.

220 See also "Guidelines on Data Protection Impact Assessment (DPIA) and determining whether processing is 'likely to result in a high risk' for the purposes of Regulation 2016/679" (Article 29 Data Protection Working Party, 2017).

Data processors, for their part, have additional obligations to inform or consult with the relevant data controller in the event of a personal data breach[221] or the appointment of a new sub-processor.[222]

8.1.2 Direct Marketing and Cookies

Sitting alongside UK data protection legislation and equally within the FCA's purview are the PECR. Among other provisions, PECR contains important restrictions on:

- unsolicited marketing by electronic means;[223] and
- storing or gaining access to "*information stored in the terminal equipment of a subscriber or user*" (*i.e.*, using cookies).[224]

Like GDPR, PECR is aimed broadly at the protection of privacy; however, the types of data within scope of PECR go beyond personal data, and PECR may apply even where a firm cannot identify the relevant person being contacted.[225]

8.1.3 Chinese Walls

A firm is entitled under SYSC 10.2.2R(1) to implement a "**Chinese wall**", defined as "*an arrangement that requires information held by a person in the course of carrying on one part of the business to be withheld*

---

221 GDPR art. 33(2).

222 GDPR art. 28(2).

223 PECR rr. 19 to 23.

224 PECR r. 6(1).

225 "Guide to Privacy and Electronic Communications Regulations" (ICO webpage, undated).

from, or not to be used for, persons with or for whom it acts in the course of carrying on another part of its business".[226]

Establishing and maintaining a Chinese wall can help a firm to demonstrate that information flow is properly controlled and thus rebut allegations of knowledge-based misconduct including certain market manipulation, conduct of business and conflict of interest breaches.[227] "**Maintaining**", for these purposes, "*includes taking reasonable steps to ensure that the arrangements remain effective and are adequately monitored*".[228]

8.1.4 Insider Lists

Where a firm acts for (or is itself) an issuer of financial instruments, it must comply with MA Reg art. 18 which requires insider lists to be drawn up, kept updated and promptly provided to the FCA upon request.[229]

8.2 Business Continuity

A firm must "*establish, implement and maintain an adequate business continuity policy aimed at ensuring, in the case of an interruption to their systems and procedures, the preservation of essential data and functions, and the maintenance of investment services and activities, or, where that is not*

226 The FCA's use of the term "Chinese wall" is not without controversy, having been described by one Californian appellate judge as "*not even an architecturally accurate metaphor for the barrier to communication created to preserve confidentiality. Such a barrier functions as a hermetic seal to prevent two-way communication between two groups. The Great Wall of China, on the other hand, was only a one-way barrier. It was built to keep outsiders out – not to keep insiders in*" (*Peat, Marwick, Mitchell & Co. v Superior Court*, 245 Cal. Rptr. (App. 1988)).

227 SYSC 10.2.3G, 4R.

228 SYSC 10.2.2R(3).

229 MA Reg ITS prescribes the precise format of such lists.

possible, the timely recovery of such data and functions and the timely resumption of their investment services and activities".[230]

For more systemically important firms including enhanced scope SMCR firms,[231] the FCA has published finalised rules which mandate, from March 2022, the identification of the firms' important business services, setting of impact tolerances for the maximum tolerable disruption, mapping and testing to a level of sophistication necessary to achieve the foregoing, and identification of any vulnerabilities in their operational resilience. By March 2025, such firms must have (1) performed mapping and testing so that they are able to remain within impact tolerances for each important business service, and (2) made the necessary investments to enable them to operate consistently within their impact tolerances. The rules will be contained mainly in a new SYSC 15A, and are part of a programme of work being carried out by the FCA in partnership with the Bank of England and the PRA.[232]

As an area of global and not just domestic importance, cyber resilience is the subject of a toolkit that has been issued by the Financial Stability Board, an international body that monitors and makes recommendations about the global financial system, and whose members include the Bank of England, the FCA and HM Treasury.[233]

8.3 Algo/HFT

A firm which engages in algorithmic trading must, most notably:

---

230 MiFID Org Regulation art. 21(3); SYSC 4.1.6R, 8G.

231 See §4.2.

232 "Building operational resilience: Feedback to CP19/32 and final rules" (PS21/3).

233 "Effective Practices for Cyber Incident Response and Recovery: Final Report" (Financial Stability Board, 2020).

- have in place suitable and effective systems and controls to ensure the resilience and other technical specifications of its trading systems;[234]

- if also a member/participant of a trading venue, immediately notify the relevant regulators that it engages in algorithmic trading;[235] and

- keep prescribed records in relation to its algorithmic trading strategies and any high-frequency algorithmic trading techniques engaged.[236]

8.4 Benchmarks Continuity

A firm that is a "**supervised entity**" within the Benchmarks Regulation (defined to include MiFID investment firms among others)[237] must comply with various regulatory requirements to the extent that it uses benchmarks.[238]

---

234 MAR 7A.3.2R, 3R.

235 MAR 7A.3.6R.

236 MAR 7A.3.7R, 8R.

237 Benchmarks Regulation art. 3(1)(17)(b).

238 "**Use of a benchmark**" means: "*(a) issuance of a financial instrument which references an index or a combination of indices; (b) determination of the amount payable under a financial instrument or a financial contract by referencing an index or a combination of indices; (c) being a party to a financial contract which references an index or a combination of indices; (d) providing a borrowing rate as defined in point (j) of Article 3 of Directive 2008/48/EC calculated as a spread or mark-up over an index or a combination of indices and that is solely used as a reference in a financial contract to which the creditor is a party; (e) measuring the performance of an investment fund through an index or a combination of indices for the purpose of tracking the return of such index or combination of indices, of defining the asset*

Key requirements for such firms include (in summary):

- produce and maintain robust written plans setting out the actions that the firm would take in the event that a benchmark materially changes or ceases to be provided;
- reflect such plans in contractual relationships with clients;[239] and
- use a benchmark only if it is on the FCA register or is provided by an administrator who is on the FCA register and located in the United Kingdom.[240]

8.4.1 Critical Benchmarks and LIBOR Transition

Benchmarks meeting certain quantitative thresholds may be deemed to be "critical benchmarks" under art. 20. In such cases, the FCA has specific powers to intervene by (most notably) prohibiting use of the benchmark by supervised entities (subject to exceptions) (art. 21A), or designating the benchmark as "unrepresentative" or "representativeness

---

allocation of a portfolio, or of computing the performance fees" (Benchmarks Regulation art. 3(1)(7)).

"**Financial instrument**" means "*any of the instruments specified in Part 1 of Schedule 2 to the Regulated Activities Order for which a request for admission to trading on a UK trading venue has been made, or which is traded on a UK trading venue or via a systematic internaliser as defined in Article 2(1)(12) of the Markets in Financial Instruments Regulation*" (Benchmarks Regulation art. 3(1)(16)).

"**Index**" means "*any figure: (a) that is published or made available to the public; (b) that is regularly determined: (i) entirely or partially by the application of a formula or any other method of calculation, or by an assessment; and (ii) on the basis of the value of one or more underlying assets or prices, including estimated prices, actual or estimated interest rates, quotes and committed quotes, or other values or surveys*" (Benchmarks Regulation art. 3(1)(1)).

239 Benchmarks Regulation art. 28(2).

240 Benchmarks Regulation art. 29(1). The Third Country Benchmarks Register and Benchmarks Administrators Register are located in the "Other Registers" section of the FS Register.

at risk" and permitting legacy use by supervised entities only in certain circumstances (arts. 23A and 23C).

Currently, the only critical benchmark in the UK is the London Inter-Bank Offered Rate ("**LIBOR**"). However, as one of a class of global benchmarks that are traditionally set by panel banks and demonstrably vulnerable to manipulation and unrepresentativeness, LIBOR has since 2014 been the subject of international efforts to transition away from inter-bank offered rates towards alternative "risk-free" rates.[241]

As part of this effort, certain versions of LIBOR ceased on 31 December 2021 by agreement with the relevant panel banks – namely, all tenors of EUR and CHF LIBOR, as well as specified tenors of USD, GBP and JPY LIBOR.

For the remaining versions of LIBOR, the FCA has decided that these should continue in some limited or altered form for a temporary period beyond that date in order to reduce disruption in the case of so-called "tough legacy" contracts. The FCA has exercised its art. 21A powers (in relation to the remaining tenors of USD LIBOR) and arts. 23A and 23C powers (in relation to the remaining tenors of GBP and JPY LIBOR) to enable this.

The latest information on this evolving situation is available at "LIBOR transition" (webpage, 2021).

8.5 Outsourcing

8.5.1 Scope and General Requirements

"**Outsourcing**" is defined as "*an arrangement of any form between a firm and a service provider by which that service provider performs a process, a service or an activity which would otherwise be undertaken by the firm itself*".

241 "Benchmarks Regulation and amendments under the Financial Services Act 2021" (document, 2021).

A firm must:

- when relying on a third party for the performance of operational functions which are critical[242] for the performance of regulated activities on a continuous and satisfactory basis, ensure that it takes reasonable steps to avoid undue additional operational risk; and

- not undertake the outsourcing of important operational functions in such a way as to impair materially:

    - the quality of its internal control; and

    - the ability of the FCA to monitor the firm's compliance with all obligations under the regulatory system and, if different, of a competent authority to monitor the firm's compliance with all obligations under MiFID.[243]

---

242 MiFID Org Regulation art. 30:

(1) … an operational function shall be regarded as critical or important where a defect or failure in its performance would materially impair the continuing compliance of an investment firm with the conditions and obligations of its authorisation or its other obligations under [MiFID], or its financial performance, or the soundness or the continuity of its investment services and activities.

(2): … the following functions shall not be considered as critical or important for the purposes of paragraph 1:

(a) the provision to the firm of advisory services, and other services which do not form part of the investment business of the firm, including the provision of legal advice to the firm, the training of personnel of the firm, billing services and the security of the firm's premises and personnel;

(b) the purchase of standardised services, including market information services and the provision of price feeds.

243 SYSC 8.1.1R.

8.5.2 Specific Requirements for Critical or Important Outsourcings

A firm must, when outsourcing critical or important operational functions, ensure that there are no systemic changes to the firm as described in MiFID Org Regulation art. 31(1).[244]

Further, a firm must exercise due skill, care and diligence when entering into, managing or terminating any arrangement for the outsourcing to a service provider of critical or important operational functions, and must take the necessary steps to ensure that the twelve conditions listed at MiFID Org Regulation art. 31(2) – relating to such matters as suitability of the service provider, supervision of outsourced functions and outsourcing resilience planning – are satisfied.[245]

A firm must ensure that the respective rights and obligations are clearly allocated and set out in a written agreement. In particular, an outsourcer must keep its instruction and termination rights, its rights of information, and its rights to carry out inspections and have access to books and premises. The agreement must ensure that any sub-

---

244 Namely:

(a) the outsourcing does not result in the delegation by senior management of its responsibility;

(b) the relationship and obligations of the investment firm towards its clients under the terms of UK law on markets in financial instruments is not altered;

(c) the conditions with which the investment firm must comply in order to have permission under Part 4A of FSMA to carry on a regulated activity which is any of the investment services and activities (within the meaning of [the Financial Services and Markets Act 2000 (Markets in Financial Instruments) Regulations 2017 r. 2(1)], and to remain so, are not undermined;

(d) none of the other conditions subject to which the firm's authorisation was granted is removed or modified.

245 Outsourcing resilience planning is an area of particular concern to the FCA. Useful materials for preparing an outsourcing resilience plan include "Outsourcing in the Asset Management Industry: Thematic Project Findings Report" (TR13/10) and "An industry response to the FSA's Dear CEO Letter on Outsourcing" (Outsourcing Working Group, 2016).

outsourcing by the service provider only takes place with the consent, in writing, of the outsourcer.[246]

Where a firm outsources functions related to the investment service of portfolio management to a service provider located in a third country, it must ensure that the following conditions are satisfied:

- the service provider is authorised or registered in its home country to provide that service and is effectively supervised by a competent authority in that third country; and

- there is an appropriate cooperation agreement[247] between the competent authority of the investment firm and the supervisory authority of the service provider.[248]

A firm "*should notify the FCA when it intends to rely on a third party for the performance of operational functions which are critical or important for the performance of relevant services and activities on a continuous and satisfactory basis*" – that is, where outsourcing services are "*of such importance that weakness, or failure, of the services would cast serious doubt upon the firm's continuing satisfaction of the threshold conditions or compliance with the Principles*".[249]

8.5.3 Guidance for Non-Critical/Important Outsourcings

SYSC 4.1.1R requires a firm to have effective processes to identify, manage, monitor and report risks and internal control mechanisms. Where a firm outsources a function that is not critical or important for the performance of relevant services and activities on a continuous and satisfactory basis, it should take into account, in a manner that is

---

246 MiFID Org Regulation art. 31(3).

247 "**Cooperation agreements**" for this purpose are listed in "Outsourcing of Portfolio Management – List of Cooperation Agreements" (document, 2018).

248 MiFID Org Regulation art. 32(1).

249 SYSC 8.1.12G; SUP 15.3.8G.

proportionate given the nature, scale and complexity of the outsourcing, the rules in SYSC 8 in complying with SYSC 4.1.1R. [250]

There is further relevant material in the EBA's "Final Report on EBA Guidelines on outsourcing arrangements" (EBA/GL/2019/02) and the FCA's "Guidance for firms outsourcing to the 'cloud' and other third-party IT services" (FG16/5).

8.6 Record-Keeping

8.6.1 Minimum List of Records

Firms must maintain adequate and orderly records of their business and internal organisation,[251] including all services, activities and transactions undertaken by it.[252]

The records must be:

- sufficient to enable the FCA to fulfil its supervisory tasks and to perform its enforcement actions, and in particular to ascertain that the firm has complied with all relevant obligations;[253]
- retained by a common platform firm in relation to its MiFID business for a period of at least 5 years;[254] and
- retained in a medium, form and manner that comply with the conditions in MiFID Org Regulation art. 72(1) relating to

[250] SYSC 8.1.3G. Functions not considered as "critical or important" for these purposes include those described in MiFID Org Reg art. 30(2) (see footnote 242).

[251] MiFID Org Regulation art. 21(1)(f).

[252] SYSC 9.1.1AR.

[253] SYSC 9.1.1AR(2).

[254] SYSC 9.1.2R.

accessibility, ascertainment of corrections and amendments, security, and usability.

Further, FCA guidance provides that generally records relating to business carried on from an establishment in the UK should be capable of being reproduced in the English language on paper or, at least, the firm should be able to provide a translation on request.[255]

MiFID Org Regulation art. 72(2) requires that firms retain at least the following records (listed in MiFID Org Regulation Annex I), depending upon the nature of their activities:

Nature of obligation	**Type of record**	**Legislative ref.**[256]
Client assessment	Information to clients	MiFID Org Regulation arts. 44 to 51
	Client agreements	MiFID Org Regulation art. 58
	Assessment of suitability and appropriateness	MiFID Org Regulation arts. 54 to 56
Order handling	Client order-handling — Aggregated transactions	MiFID Org Regulation arts. 67 to 70
	Aggregation and allocation of transactions for own account	MiFID Org Regulation art. 69

255 SYSC 9.1.4G.

256 Some of the legislative references given here are updated from those in the official text of the MiFID Org Regulation.

Client orders and transactions	Record keeping of client orders or decision to deal	MiFID Org Regulation art. 74
	Record keeping of transactions and order processing	MiFID Org Regulation art. 75
Reporting to clients	Obligation in respect of services provided to clients	MiFID Org Regulation arts. 59 to 63
Safeguarding of client assets	Client financial instruments held by an investment firm	CASS 6.6.2R to 4R
	Client funds held by an investment firm	CASS 7.15.2R, 3R
	Use of client financial instruments	CASS 6.4.3R
Communication with clients	Information about costs and associated charges	MiFID Org Regulation art. 50
	Information about the investment firm and its services, financial instruments and safeguarding of client assets	MiFID Org Regulation arts. 47 to 49
	Information to clients	MiFID Org Regulation art. 44
	Marketing communications (except in oral form)	MiFID Org Regulation arts. 36, 37
	Investment advice to retail clients	MiFID Org Regulation art. 54
	Investment research	MiFID Org Regulation arts. 36, 37

Organisational requirements	The firm's business and internal organisation	MiFID Org Regulation art. 21(1)(f)
	Compliance reports	MiFID Org Regulation arts. 22(2)(c), 25(2)
	Conflict of Interest record	MiFID Org Regulation art. 35
	Inducements	COBS 2.3A.32R
	Risk management reports	MiFID Org Regulation arts. 23(2)(b), 25(2)
	Internal audit reports	MiFID Org Regulation arts. 24, 25(2)
	Complaints-handling records	MiFID Org Regulation art. 26
	Records of personal transactions	MiFID Org Regulation art. 29(5)(c)

Outside of MiFID Org Regulation Annex I, there are numerous additional requirements (or quasi-requirements) to maintain specific books and records, including:

	Type of record	Legislative ref.
Systems and controls	Policies and procedures required to be maintained under the MiFID and MA Reg frameworks	MiFID Org Regulation art. 72(3)
	Compliance risk assessment and compliance monitoring programme	MiFID Org Regulation art. 22(2)
	Decision-making procedures and organisational structure, including reporting lines and allocation of functions and responsibilities	MiFID Org Regulation art. 21(1)(a)
	Outsourcing and outsourcing resilience	MiFID Org Regulation art. 31; SYSC 8
	Conflicts of interest register	MiFID Org Regulation art. 35; SYSC 10
	Appointed representatives and tied agents	SUP 12.9.1R, 5R
	Financial crime risk assessment	FCG 2.2.4
	ICARA document and its review and approval by the firm's governing body	MIFIDPRU 7.8.10R
	Benchmarks contingency plan	Benchmarks Regulation art. 28
	Data processing activities	GDPR art. 30
	Compliance breaches, issues identified, and follow-up actions	MiFID Org Regulation art. 22(2)(a)

	Periodic and *ad hoc* correspondence with regulators	Principle 11
	Accounting records	MiFID Org Regulation art. 21(4)
Clients and investors	Product governance target market	PROD 3
	Customer due diligence documentation	MLR r. 40
	Use of client asset mandates	CASS 8.3.1R
Senior management and staff	Technical training and competence	MiFID Org Regulation art. 21(1)(d)
	Compliance training	MiFID Org Regulation art. 22(2)(b)
	SMF managers' statements of responsibilities (current and past versions)	SUP 10C.11.20R, 22G
	Remuneration Code material risk takers	SYSC 19G.5.2R
	Steps taken to comply with the handover material rules, and comprehensive and up-to-date management responsibilities map (Enhanced scope SMCR firms only)	SYSC 25.9.5R, 25.2.1R(1)
	Certification employees	SYSC 27.2.13G
	Approved persons	FSMA s. 59(1)

	Gifts, entertainment and acceptable non-monetary benefits	Bribery Act 2010 s. 7(2); MiFID Org Regulation art. 33; COBS 2.3A.5R
	Research received within exemption from prohibition against inducements	COBS 2.3A.5R
Trading	Telephone conversations and electronic communications in relation to stipulated activities in financial instruments	SYSC 10A.1.6R
	Derivative contracts concluded (whether OTC (over-the-counter) or listed), and any modifications	EMIR art. 9(2)
	Algorithms used	MAR 7A.3.8R
	Insider lists	MA Reg art. 18
	Trade errors	COBS 2.1.1R(1); MA Reg RTS art. 2(1)
	Engagement policy (Certain types of firm only, including UK firms providing portfolio management services, UK UCITS management companies and full-scope UK AIFMs)	COBS 2.2B.5R to 7R
	Best execution	COBS 11.2A.31R
	Suspicious transaction and order reports ("**STORs**") and analysis performed on suspicious transactions and orders which did not result in submission of a STOR	MA Reg RTS recital 12

	Transactions and orders modified, cancelled or rejected (as well as executed/placed), and any other relevant market conduct data that would "cover the full range of trading activities undertaken"	MA Reg RTS art. 2(1), 3
	Market soundings	MA Reg art. 11
	Relevant data in relation to orders and transactions, and portfolio compressions	MiFIR arts. 25, 31

Firms should also refer to the record-keeping requirements summarised in Schedule 1 to each module in the FCA Handbook.[257]

8.6.2 Recording Telephone Conversations and Electronic Communications

UK MiFID investment firms must:

- take all reasonable steps to record telephone conversations, and keep a copy of electronic communications, relating to managing investments (among other activities), that are made with, sent from, or received on, equipment that is provided or permitted by the firm;[258]

- take all reasonable steps to prevent an employee or contractor from making, sending, or receiving relevant telephone conversations and electronic communications on privately-owned equipment which the firm is unable to record or copy;[259]

---

[257] SYSC 9.1.6G.

[258] SYSC 10A.1.6R.

[259] SYSC 10A.1.7R.

- educate and train employees in procedures governing the above rules;[260] and

- periodically monitor the records of transactions and orders subject to the communications recording requirements, including relevant conversations, taking a risk-based and proportionate approach.[261]

Records must be kept for a period of 5 years or, where requested by the FCA, for a period of up to 7 years.[262]

There is an exemption under SYSC 10A.1.9R for MiFID optional exemption firms (such as many independent financial advisers) that provide services solely or mainly to retail clients. Such firms may, instead of recording relevant telephone conversations, keep a written minute or note, provided that it captures all relevant information including at least:

- date and time of the conversation;

- identity of the individual participants in the conversation;

- initiator of the conversation; and

- relevant information about the client order, including the price, volume, type of order and when it will be transmitted or executed.

---

260 MiFID Org Regulation art. 76(5).

261 MiFID Org Regulation art. 76(6).

262 SYSC 10A.1.14R.

To the extent that a firm will record calls, it must notify new and existing clients accordingly before the provision of an investment service,[263] and must in any case make all reasonable efforts to inform callers generally.[264]

263 SYSC 10A.1.11R.

264 Telecommunications (Lawful Business Practice) (Interception of Communications) Regulations 2000.

9 FINANCIAL CONTROLS

A firm's handling of its own assets and those of its clients is subject to important restrictions designed to ensure the financial safety and soundness of the firm and adequate protection for its customers' accounts.

9.1 Capital Requirements: MIFIDPRU Investment Firms

Principle 4 states: "*A firm must maintain adequate financial resources.*"

For many firms the concept of "adequacy" of financial resources is delineated in MIFIDPRU, which is the prudential sourcebook that applies to MIFIDPRU investment firms and came into force in January 2022.[265]

"**MIFIDPRU investment firm**" has the same meaning as "**FCA investment firm**" as defined in FSMA s. 143A, and includes any investment firm that is an authorised person that has its registered office (or, if it has no registered office, its head office) in the UK, other than (in summary) dual-regulated firms and "article 3" and "article 2" MiFID exempt firms (see §3.2.1).

A MIFIDPRU investment firm is deemed to be small and non-interconnected, and is defined as an "**SNI MIFIDPRU investment firm**", if it satisfies all of the conditions set out in MIFIDPRU 1.2.1R.[266]

---

265 As MIFIDPRU covers a wide range of firms which until recently came within disparate predecessor regimes (such as former "BIPRU firms", "exempt CAD firms" and "IFPRU firms"), firms should note that important transitional provisions are set out at MIFIDPRU TP 1 to TP 12.

266 In summary: average assets under management < £1.2 billion; average client orders handled < £100 million per day (cash trades) and £1 billion per day

All other MIFIDPRU investment firms are referred to as "**non-SNI MIFIDPRU investment firms**". SNI MIFIDPRU investment firms enjoy various carveouts from MIFIDPRU rules governing capital and liquidity requirements, remuneration, and regulatory reporting and public disclosures.

A MIFIDPRU investment firm that is a clearing member or an indirect clearing firm should refer to supplemental rules in MIFIDPRU 7.10.

Finally, a firm that is a member of a group should note that there are detailed rules in MIFIDPRU governing prudential consolidation that are beyond the scope of this book.

9.1.1 Own Funds Requirement

Under the "**own funds requirement**" as specified in MIFIDPRU 4.3, MIFIDPRU investment firms must at all times maintain own funds that are the highest of:

- its "**permanent minimum capital requirement**" as defined in MIFIDPRU 4.4;[267]
- its "**fixed overheads requirement**" as defined in MIFIDPRU 4.5;[268] or

(derivatives trades); average assets safeguarded and administered = zero; average client money held = zero; does not have permission to deal on own account; on- and off-balance sheet total < £100 million; total two-year average annual gross revenue from investment services and/or activities < £30 million; not a clearing member or an indirect clearing firm; and average daily trading flow = zero.

267 This is set by the FCA at £750,000, £150,000 or £75,000, depending upon the firm's regulatory permissions.

268 This is, in summary, an amount equal to one quarter of the firm's relevant expenditure during the preceding year.

- (in the case of non-SNI MIFIDPRU investment firms only) its "**K-factor requirement**" as defined in MIFIDPRU 4.6.

A firm's "**own funds**" comprise the sum of its common equity tier 1 capital, additional tier 1 capital, and tier 2 capital. As well as having own funds that are at least equal to the own funds requirement, the firm's common equity tier 1 capital must be at least 56% of the own funds requirement, and the sum of its common equity tier 1 capital and additional tier 1 capital must be at least 75% of the own funds requirement.[269]

Where relevant (*i.e.*, for non-SNI MIFIDPRU investment firms), the K-factor requirement is the sum of each of the following components as may be applicable to the firm:

Component	Summary	MIFIDPRU ref.
K-AUM requirement	0.02% of the firm's average assets under management.	4.7
K-CMH requirement	The sum of: 0.4% of average client money held by the firm in segregated accounts; and 0.5% of average client money held by the firm in non-segregated accounts.	4.8
K-ASA requirement	0.04% of the firm's average assets safeguarded and administered.	4.9
K-COH requirement	The sum of: 0.1% of average client orders handled attributable to cash trades; and 0.01% of average client orders handled attributable to derivatives trades.	4.10

269 MIFIDPRU 3.2.1R, 2R.

K-NPR requirement *	Requirement based on net position risk. Calculated in accordance with UK CRR, Part Three Title IV as at 31 December 2021.	4.11, 4.12
K-CMG requirement *	Requirement based on clearing margin given. Equal to TM * 1.3, where "**TM**" is the third highest amount of total margin required from the firm on a daily basis over the preceding 3 months.	4.11, 4.13
K-TCD requirement *	Requirement based on trading counterparty default risk. Equal to α * EV * RF * CVA, where: α = 1.2; EV = exposure value; RF = risk factor applicable to the counterparty type; and CVA = the credit valuation adjustment.	4.11, 4.14
K-DTF requirement *	The sum of: 0.1% of average daily trading flow attributable to cash trades; and 0.01% of average daily trading flow attributable to derivatives trades.	4.11, 4.15
K-CON requirement	Requirement based on concentration risk. Equal to the sum of the "CON own funds requirement" for each client or group of connected clients for which the exposure value exceeds the concentration risk soft limit.	4.11, 4.16, 5.7

Note that the requirements marked with an asterisk only apply to a firm that deals on own account (whether on its own behalf or on behalf of its clients); the K-DTF requirement, additionally, applies to a firm that executes orders on behalf of clients in the firm's own name.[270]

270 MIFIDPRU 4.11.4R, 5R.

9.1.2 Basic Liquid Assets Requirement

Under the "**basic liquid assets requirement**" contained in MIFIDPRU 6.2.1R, a firm must hold an amount of core liquid assets equal to the sum of one third of the amount of its fixed overhead requirement and 1.6% of the total amount of any guarantees provided to clients.

"**Core liquid assets**" include (most notably) sterling-denominated short-term deposits at a UK-authorised credit institution, assets representing claims on or guaranteed by the UK Government or the Bank of England, and units or shares in a short-term regulated money market fund.[271]

9.1.3 Overall Financial Adequacy Rule, ICARA and SREP

In addition to the primary own funds requirement and the basic liquid assets requirement, MIFIDPRU investment firms must, further, comply with the "**overall financial adequacy rule**" set out at MIFIDPRU 7.4.7R(1) which states that:

> *A firm must, at all times, hold own funds and liquid assets which are adequate, both as to their amount and their quality, to ensure that:*
>
> *(a) the firm is able to remain financially viable throughout the economic cycle, with the ability to address any material potential harm that may result from its ongoing activities; and*
>
> *(b) the firm's business can be wound down in an orderly manner, minimising harm to consumers or to other market participants.*

The supplemental requirements imposed by the overall financial adequacy rule are designed to account for the reality that "*the amount and quality of own funds and liquid assets that each firm must hold will vary*

[271] MIFIDPRU 6.3.1R.

according to its business model and operating model, the environment in which it operates and the nature of its internal systems and controls".[272]

The amounts of own funds and liquid assets that a firm needs to hold in order to comply with the overall financial adequacy rule are referred to as the "**own funds threshold requirement**" and "**liquid assets threshold requirement**" respectively. The rules for calculating these amounts are set out in MIFIDPRU 7.6 and 7.7, and form part of a wider obligation on firms to maintain an internal capital adequacy and risk assessment ("**ICARA**") process as required by MIFIDPRU 7.4.9R.

The FCA describes the ICARA process as "*the collective term for the internal systems and controls that a firm must operate to identify and manage potential material harms that may arise from the operation of its business, and to ensure that its operations can be wound down in an orderly manner*".[273] Detailed specifications for a firm's ICARA process are contained in MIFIDPRU 7.4 to 7.9.

A firm must review the adequacy of the ICARA process at least once every 12 months and following any material change in business model or operating model.[274] All such reviews must be documented, and the resulting "**ICARA document**" must be reviewed and approved by the firm's governing body; adequate records of both the ICARA document and its review and approval must be retained for at least 3 years from the date of approval.[275]

A firm's ICARA process may be scrutinised directly by the FCA through a supervisory review and evaluation process ("**SREP**"). The FCA may conduct an SREP on a specific firm's ICARA process or may conduct a thematic review of a sector in which multiple firms are active;[276] further

---

272 MIFIDPRU 7.4.8G(1).

273 MIFIDPRU 7.4.8G(2).

274 MIFIDPRU 7.8.2R.

275 MIFIDPRU 7.8.7R, 8R, 10R.

276 MIFIDPRU 7.4.8G(6).

guidance on how the FCA normally conducts an SREP is contained in MIFIDPRU 7.10.

9.1.4 Financial Regulatory Reporting, Notifications and Disclosures

For an outline of reports and notifications that MIFIDPRU investment firms must submit to the FCA, see §5.2 and §5.3.

For an outline of disclosures that MIFIDPRU investment firms must publish, see §12.1.

9.2 Capital Requirements: Other Types of Firms

Certain types of firms should be aware of additional or alternative capital requirements contained elsewhere in the FCA Handbook. Some notable sets of requirements are set out below:

Type of firm	Summary of scope	FCA Handbo ok ref.
Firms that are members of financial conglomerates	"**Financial conglomerate**" is defined at GENPRU 3 Annex 4R as, essentially, a consolidation group with at least one of its members being within the insurance sector and at least one within the banking sector or investment services sector, and satisfying certain financial conditions.	GENPR U 3
IFPRU 730k firms not subject to supervision on a consolidated basis (and certain group entities)	"**IFPRU 730k firms**" are firms that have the highest possible initial capital requirement because their activities are not subject to any of the limitations that would have brought them within a lower prudential category. Because of their significance within the financial system, IFPRU 730k firms are subject to detailed recovery and resolution planning requirements.	IFPRU 11

Certain insurers	"**Insurers**" are firms with permission to effect or carry out contracts of insurance.	INSPRU ; IPRU-INS
Mortgage and home finance firms, and insurance intermediaries	Relevant for firms that have permission to carry on insurance distribution activity, home finance mediation activity, home financing, home finance administration or insurance business.	MIPRU
Friendly societies	"**Friendly societies**" are societies incorporated under the Friendly Societies Act 1992 or registered under the Friendly Societies Act 1974 (or predecessor Act).	IRPU-FSOC
Certain securities and futures firms	"**Securities and futures firms**" (defined as including energy market participants, oil market participants and other narrow categories of firms) that are not MiFID investment firms.	IPRU-INV 3
Collective portfolio management firms	"**Collective portfolio management firms**" comprise UCITS managers and AIFMs. Collective portfolio management firms that have additional MiFID permissions are referred to as "**collective portfolio management investment firms**", and are additionally subject to MIFIDPRU.[277]	IPRU-INV 11
Operators of electronic systems in relation to lending	Relevant for persons who have, or ought to have, permission for operating an electronic system in relation to lending.	IPRU-INV 12

277 MIFIDPRU 1.1.2G.

Debt management firms	Firms which carry on "debt counselling" or "debt adjusting" where they (or an associate, if together they carry on both activities) intend for an individual to enter into a particular debt solution.	CONC 10

Finally, dual-regulated firms, including designated investment firms, are prudentially regulated by the PRA within a complex framework that originated in the EU's fourth Capital Requirements Directive ("**CRD IV**") and is set out in the PRA Rulebook.

9.3 Remuneration

9.3.1 MIFIDPRU Remuneration Code

MIFIDPRU investment firms must comply with the MIFIDPRU Remuneration Code which is set out at SYSC 19G.

As detailed in SYSC 19G.1.1R to 6R, precisely which set of MIFIDPRU Remuneration Code provisions applies to a MIFIDPRU investment firm depends upon whether the firm is classified as:

(1) an SNI MIFIDPRU investment firm – for which, <u>basic</u> remuneration requirements are applicable;

(2) a non-SNI MIFIDPRU investment firm falling within SYSC 19G.1.1R(2)[278] – for which, <u>standard</u> remuneration requirements are applicable; or

[278] SYSC 19G.1.1R(2) prescribes the following quantitative ceilings to distinguish between these two types of non-SNI MIFIDPRU investment firms: (a) where the value of the firm's on-balance sheet assets and off-balance sheet items over the preceding 4-year period is a rolling average of £100 million or less; or (b) where: (i) the value of the firm's on-balance sheet assets and off-balance sheet items over

(3) a non-SNI MIFIDPRU investment firm not falling within SYSC 19G.1.1R(2) – for which, extended remuneration requirements are applicable.

Below is a synopsis of the operative requirements in SYSC 19G and their scope:

SYSC 19G ref.	**Summary of requirements**	**Basic remuneration requirements?**	**Standard remuneration requirements?**	**Extended remuneration requirements?**
2	• Remuneration policies and practices	Yes	Yes	Yes
3.1R to 3.3R and 3.6R to 3.8G	• Oversight of remuneration policies and practices • Control functions	Yes	Yes	Yes
4.1R to 4.5R and 4.7G	• Fixed and variable components of remuneration	Yes	Yes	Yes
6.1R to 2R (and 3G), and 6.5R to 6.6G	• Remuneration and capital	Yes	Yes	Yes

---

the preceding 4-year period is a rolling average of £300 million or less; and (ii) the conditions in (3) are (where they are relevant to a firm) satisfied. The conditions in (3) are: (a) that the exposure value of the firm's on- and off-balance sheet trading book business is equal to or less than £150 million; and (b) that the exposure value of the firm's on- and off-balance sheet derivatives business is equal to or less than £100 million.

	• Exceptional government intervention • Assessment of performance			
3.4R to 3.5G	• Internal review of implementation of remuneration policies and practices	No	Yes	Yes
4.6R and 4.8R to 4.12G	• Setting ratio between variable and fixed components of remuneration*	No	Yes	Yes
5.1R to 5.8G and 5.13G	• Application to material risk takers – identification	No	Yes	Yes
6.4R, 6.7R to 6.18R, 6.30R to 6.35R(1) and 6.36R to 6.38R	• Assessment of performance – supplemental rules • General requirements for awards of non-standard forms of variable remuneration • Guaranteed variable remuneration* • Retention awards* • Severance pay* • Buy-out awards*	No	Yes	Yes

	• Risk adjustment • Performance adjustment* • Discretionary pension benefits* • Personal investment strategies* • Avoidance of the MIFIDPRU Remuneration Code			
7	• Remuneration committee	No	No[279]	Yes
5.9R to 5.12G	• Application to material risk takers – exemption for individuals	No	No[280]	Yes
6.19R (including Annex 1) to 6.29R and 6.35R(2)	• Shares, instruments and alternative arrangements* • Retention policy* • Deferral* • Discretionary pension benefits – supplemental rules*	No	No	Yes

[279] Effectively excluded by virtue of MIFIDPRU 7.1.4R.

[280] Effectively excluded by virtue of SYSC 19G.5.10G.

Certain of the standard and extended remuneration requirements, marked in the table above with an asterisk, are stated to apply only to a firm's "material risk takers" (although firms are encouraged to consider applying them to other members of staff also).[281]

A "**material risk taker**" is defined at SYSC 19G.5.1R as "*a staff member at a non-SNI MIFIDPRU investment firm whose professional activities have a material impact on the risk profile of the firm or of the assets that the firm manages*", and various types of staff member to be included or excluded from scope are described in the remainder of SYSC 19G.5. Under SYSC 19G.5.2R, "*A non-SNI MIFIDPRU investment firm must assess at least once a year which of its staff members are material risk takers*", and the FCA publishes a template to enable firms to record the assessment.[282]

A key aspect of the rules applicable to material risk takers is performance adjustment, and on this topic firms should refer to the FCA's "General guidance on the application of ex-post risk adjustment to variable remuneration" (FG21/5).

Finally, a fundamental obligation on every MIFIDPRU investment firm is to "*ensure that its remuneration policies and practices (including performance assessment processes and decisions) are clear and*

281 SYSC 19G.5.13G. Regarding setting a ratio between variable and fixed components of remuneration: note that MIFIDPRU 19G.4.7G(1) appears to contemplate that all staff including material risk takers are caught. However, the FCA has published webinar slides clarifying that "*This requirement applies... only in relation to those members of staff identified as material risk takers (MRTs)*". See "Investment Firms Prudential Regime – Webinar 2: Practical Implementation (30 November 2021)" (document, 2021).

282 "MIFIDPRU Remuneration Code Remuneration Policy Statement (RPS) Table: MRTs list" (document, 2021). Firms should note that a material risk taker is likely also to be performing an FCA certification function (see §4.4.1).

documented",[283] and the FCA has made a template document available to assist with this process.[284]

9.3.2 Other Remuneration Regimes

Firms that are AIFMs or UCITS managers are subject to remuneration codes that have provisions roughly analogous to those of the MIFIDPRU Remuneration Code. The AIFM Remuneration Code (originally implementing AIFMD art. 13(1)) and UCITS Remuneration Code (originally implementing UCITS Directive art. 14a(1)) are set out at SYSC 19B and 19E respectively.

For CPMI firms (*i.e.*, AIFMs and/or UCITS managers that have "top-up" regulatory permission for managing investments), the MIFIDPRU Remuneration Code applies in addition to the AIFM Remuneration Code and/or UCITS Remuneration Code. Where there are conflicting remuneration requirements the most stringent provision prevails.[285]

Dual-regulated firms (*i.e.*, regulated by both the FCA and PRA) are subject to the Dual-Regulated Firms Remuneration Code in SYSC 19D, which originally transposed various EU provisions including CRD IV arts. 92 to 96.

Separately, investment firms are reminded that there are overlapping "remuneration incentive" rules in MiFID Org Regulation art. 27 and SYSC 19F, which are described in §7.2.2.

9.4 Client Assets

Principle 10 states: "*A firm must arrange adequate protection for clients' assets when it is responsible for them.*" "Clients' assets" here refers to both

283 SYSC 19G.2.3G.

284 "Remuneration Policy Statement Template – MIFIDPRU Remuneration Code (SYSC 19G)" (document, 2021).

285 SYSC 19G.1.14G and 20R.

money and financial instruments, and the rules governing their treatment are located principally in CASS.

Generally, firms that receive or hold clients' assets are classified as a "**CASS large firm**", "**CASS medium firm**" or "**CASS small firm**", depending upon the highest total value of client money or safe custody assets held during the last calendar year or projected for the current calendar year.[286] A firm that is classified as a CASS large firm or CASS medium firm must:

- ➢ allocate the CASS oversight function to a director or senior manager (who will thus be performing an FCA certification function – see §4.4.1); and
- ➢ submit monthly Client Money and Assets Returns to the FCA (see §5.2.2).

To the extent that a firm does not have permission to hold client assets, it should bear in mind that it will *prima facie* be "acting without permission" (in breach of FSMA s. 20(1)) if at any time it does end up in possession of such assets. This could occur inadvertently, for example where the firm receives an overpayment from a client. Firms are expected to have systems in place to prevent, promptly detect and appropriately deal with any such breaches, and where a firm claims not to hold client money or custody assets this will be scrutinised by the firm's auditor.[287]

9.4.1 Client Money Rules

Where a firm receives or holds money for or on behalf of a client in the course of or in connection with its MiFID and certain other types of

---

286 CASS 1A.2.7R. Respectively, the thresholds in terms of client money are >£1 billion, £1 million to £1 billion, and <£1 million, and the thresholds in terms of safe custody assets are >£100 billion, £10 million to £100 billion, and <£10 million. Firms are able to opt in to a higher category of "CASS firm type" (CASS 1A.2.5R).

287 SUP 3.10.4R(2).

regulated business ("**client money**"), the "**client money rules**" in CASS 7 may be engaged.[288]

Excluded from the scope of "client money" for these purposes is money held at a bank[289] or held pursuant to exclusions in CASS 7.11.[290]

A firm that receives and holds client money does so as trustee on the terms of a statutory trust created by CASS 7.17 (under the authority of FSMA s.137B(1)). The statutory trust includes a stipulation that the client money is held for the purposes of, and on the terms of, the client money rules.[291]

As such, the firm must (most notably):

- have organisational arrangements in place to protect client money with regard to, in particular, fraud, poor administration, inadequate record-keeping and negligence, under CASS 7.12;

---

288 A separate, lighter-touch regime exists for firms engaged in insurance mediation activity (CASS 5). Firms subject to both CASS 5 and CASS 7 may elect in writing to comply with CASS 7 in respect of all client money held (CASS 7.10.3R). Additionally, a further separate regime exists for debt management firms (CASS 11).

289 CASS 7.10.16R.

290 Those exclusions cover, most notably: certain title transfer collateral arrangements with non-retail clients; delivery versus payment transactions; money that is due and payable to the firm; commission rebates; and money in respect of which a firm's fiduciary duty has been discharged.

291 The current drafting of CASS 7.17, and of the client money distribution and transfer rules in CASS 7A and analogous rules for safe custody assets in CASS 6.7, are in large part a response to the high-profile litigation that culminated with the Supreme Court case *In the matter of Lehman Brothers International (Europe) (In Administration) and In the matter of the Insolvency Act 1986* [2012] UKSC 6. That judgment had been required in order to address lacunas in the predecessor rules regarding (1) the timing for when a statutory trust arises and (2) constitution of the client money pool upon a firm's failure.

- segregate client money from the firm's own money in accordance with CASS 7.13;
- allow third parties to hold client money only for the purposes of segregation under CASS 7.13 or in the circumstances set out in CASS 7.14, and obtain a countersigned acknowledgment letter in accordance with CASS 7.18; and
- comply with record-keeping, accounting and reconciliation requirements in CASS 7.15 and 7.16.

It is possible for a firm and its professional clients to opt out from the client money rules, but not in relation to MiFID business or insurance mediation activity.[292]

9.4.2 Custody Rules

As with the client money rules, the "**custody rules**" in CASS 6 may be engaged where a firm holds "**safe custody assets**", defined as including financial instruments in relation to MiFID business (among other types of investments).

General exclusions from the custody rules are set out in CASS 6.1.

Where applicable, the custody rules require firms to (most notably):

- have organisational arrangements in place to protect clients' safe custody assets with regard to, in particular, fraud, poor administration, inadequate record-keeping and negligence, under CASS 6.2, including following rules on the registration and recording of legal title;

[292] CASS 7.10.8R, 12R.

- comply with due diligence and other requirements when depositing (or arranging the deposit of) safe custody assets with third parties, under CASS 6.3;
- observe the restrictions on use of safe custody assets in CASS 6.4; and
- comply with record-keeping, accounting and reconciliation requirements in CASS 6.6.

9.4.3 Other CASS Regimes

CASS also includes the following regimes that are related to client money and safe custody assets:

- CASS 3 which applies "*to a firm when it receives or holds assets in connection with an arrangement to secure the obligation of a client in the course of, or in connection with*" its regulated business (*i.e.*, collateral);[293]
- CASS 8, containing rules for records and internal controls where a firm has "**mandates**": defined to include (in summary) permission from a client for the firm to control the client's assets or liabilities;[294] and
- CASS 9, which prescribes reporting, disclosure and information requirements for prime brokerage firms to whom the client money rules and/or the custody rules are applicable.

9.4.4 Auditor's CASS Report

Firms should bear in mind that the adequacy of their systems for complying with relevant CASS regimes is something that a firm's auditor

293 CASS 3.1.1R.

294 CASS 8.2.1R.

may be specifically required to opine on and report to the FCA under SUP 3.10 (if applicable – see SUP 3.1.2R).

10 THE SECOND AND THIRD LINES OF DEFENCE

The "three lines of defence" model for governance, risk management and control has been adopted by more and more organisations in recent years, not least the FCA itself.[295] Although the FCA does not explicitly mandate the "three lines of defence" model for financial firms, it noted in a review conducted in 2017 that "*[w]ithout exception, every firm in our sample operates a structure modelled on the three lines of defence*".[296]

In broad terms, the "three lines of defence" model delineates the roles within an organisation as follows:

- "first line" roles: provision of products/services to clients and managing risk;
- "second line" roles: expertise, support, monitoring and challenge on risk-related matters; and
- "third line" roles: independent and objective assurance and advice on all matters related to the achievement of objectives.[297]

In a typical firm, the first line would comprise the business functions, the second line the compliance oversight, financial crime risk oversight and risk control roles, and the third line internal audit.

---

295 "Internal Audit final report – A review of risk management and the implementation of the first and second lines of defence" (document, 2014).

296 For example, by the FCA in its report "The compliance function in wholesale banks" (document, 2017); see also "Final report – Guidelines on certain aspects of the MiFID compliance function requirements" (ESMA35-36-1946) (ESMA, 2020).

297 "The IIA's Three Lines Model: An update of the Three Lines of Defense" (Institute of Internal Auditors, 2020).

10.1 Compliance Oversight

10.1.1 Compliance Function

Under MiFID Org Regulation art. 22(2), a firm must have a permanent and effective compliance function which operates independently and has the following monitoring and advisory responsibilities:

- monitoring and assessing the adequacy and effectiveness of the firm's compliance risk detection and mitigation procedures, and the actions taken to address any deficiencies; and

- advising and assisting staff responsible for carrying out investment services and activities to comply with the firm's obligations under UK law on markets in financial instruments.

These tasks must include conducting "*an assessment on the basis of which [the firm] shall establish a risk-based monitoring programme that takes into consideration all areas of the investment firm's investment services, activities and any relevant ancillary services, including relevant information gathered in relation to the monitoring of complaints handling. The monitoring programme shall establish priorities determined by the compliance risk assessment ensuring that compliance risk is comprehensively monitored.*"

Further, the compliance function has the following reporting and complaints-related responsibilities:

- reporting to the management body, on at least an annual basis, on the implementation and effectiveness of the overall control environment for investment services and activities, on the risks that have been identified and on the complaints-handling reporting as well as remedies undertaken or to be undertaken; and

- monitoring the operations of the complaints-handling process and considering complaints as a source of relevant information in the context of its general monitoring responsibilities.

The organisational requirements of the compliance function are prescribed by MiFID Org Regulation art. 22(3) and (4), under which investment firms must ensure that:

- the compliance function has the necessary authority, resources, expertise and access to all relevant information;
- a compliance officer is appointed who is responsible for the compliance function and for submitting regular compliance reports to senior personnel;[298]
- the compliance function reports on an *ad hoc* basis directly to the management body where it detects a significant risk of failure by the firm to comply with its obligations under UK law on markets in financial instruments; and
- the following restrictions are complied with (to the extent proportionate): staff involved in the compliance function are not involved in the performance of services or activities they monitor; and the method of determining the remuneration of staff involved in the compliance function does not compromise their objectivity and is not likely to do so.[299]

As referenced in SYSC 6.1, guidelines on the compliance function's responsibilities and organisational requirements were issued by ESMA in 2012 which are still relevant.[300]

---

298 The compliance officer is likely to be performing the compliance oversight function, which is designated as a senior management function under SUP 10C.6.1R requiring FCA approval. See §4.3.2.

299 SYSC 6.1.4-AG reminds firms that the relevant remuneration code will also apply to the remuneration of relevant persons involved in the compliance function – see §9.3.

300 "Final report – Guidelines on certain aspects of the MiFID compliance function requirements" (ESMA35-36-1946) (ESMA, 2020).

More recently, in 2017 the FCA published a report into the compliance function in wholesale banks. This provides practical insights that could be of interest to investment firms, and covers: the role and structure of the compliance function; strategy and planning; compliance monitoring; technology; support and challenge; and personnel.[301]

10.1.2 Compliance Monitoring

A firm must "*establish a risk-based monitoring programme that takes into consideration all areas of the investment firm's investment services, activities and any relevant ancillary services, including relevant information gathered in relation to the monitoring of complaints handling. The monitoring programme shall establish priorities determined by the compliance risk assessment ensuring that compliance risk is comprehensively monitored*".[302]

A firm may have had to prepare a compliance monitoring programme as part of its initial authorisation application to the FCA. In principle, firms must establish their own bespoke compliance monitoring programme which covers the topics addressed in their compliance policies and procedures.

Note, however, that specific monitoring requirements are set out in MiFID Org Regulation art. 21(5), covering:

- the following organisational matters, to the extent appropriate and proportionate:
    - decision-making procedures and organisational structure;
    - relevant persons' awareness of procedures to be followed for the proper discharge of their responsibilities;
    - internal control mechanisms;

---

[301] "The compliance function in wholesale banks" (document, 2017).

[302] MiFID Org Regulation art. 22(2).

  - skills, knowledge and expertise of personnel;
  - internal reporting and communication of information;
  - records of business and internal organisation;
  - soundness, honesty and professionalism in discharge of functions by any relevant persons who have multiple functions;

- security, integrity and confidentiality of information;
- business continuity; and
- accounting policies and procedures.

Additional specific monitoring requirements include:

- The firm's compliance function must monitor the operations of the complaints-handling process and consider complaints as a source of relevant information in the context of its general monitoring responsibilities.[303]
- Firms that arrange or execute transactions must ensure "*effective and ongoing monitoring, for the purposes of detecting and identifying orders and transactions that could constitute insider dealing, market manipulation or attempted insider dealing or market manipulation*".[304]
- Firms must periodically monitor the records of transactions and orders subject to the communications recording requirements,

303 MiFID Org Regulation art. 22(2)(d).

304 MA Reg RTS art. 2(1)(a).

including relevant conversations, taking a risk-based and proportionate approach.[305]

- The requirement to "take all sufficient steps to obtain" best execution (see §11.5) requires "*firms to monitor not only the execution quality obtained but also the quality and appropriateness of their execution arrangements and policies on an ex-ante and ex-post basis to identify circumstances under which changes may be appropriate*".[306]

- Compliance monitoring of money laundering and terrorist financing policies and procedures is required under MLR r. 19(3)(e).

- Firms should monitor their information barrier arrangements, for the purposes of "maintaining" a Chinese wall.[307]

- A data protection officer (if appointed for the purposes of GDPR art. 37(1)) must monitor a firm's compliance with GDPR.[308]

- Firms must test their transaction reporting process and perform regular reconciliations of their front-office trading records against data samples provided to them by the FCA to that effect.[309] In the UK, such data samples are provided via the FCA's MDP (Market Data Processor) Entity Portal.

---

305 MiFID Org Regulation art. 76(6).

306 "Questions and Answers on MiFID II and MiFIR investor protection and intermediaries topics" (ESMA35-43-349) (ESMA, 2021); see also "Best execution and payment for order flow" (TR14/13) and "Investment managers still failing to ensure effective oversight of best execution" (webpage, 2021).

307 SYSC 10.2.2R(3).

308 GDPR art. 39(1)(b).

309 MiFID RTS 22 art. 15(3).

Finally, by way of guidance, the FCA includes, in its notes to a retail intermediary firm's authorisation application form,[310] an example of a compliance monitoring programme, which lists the following business risks and regulatory requirements:

FCA's example compliance monitoring programme for retail intermediary firm
New business records are maintained.
Financial promotions undertaken are up to date and correct. This includes stationery and terms of business letter.
Status disclosed on all stationery.
Clients are properly classified and given the appropriate range of advice.
Adequate complaints records are kept.
Adequate recruitment records are kept for new advisers.
Personal account dealing procedures are maintained.
Training and competence records are maintained (including Key Performance Indicators).
The fitness and propriety of individuals are established and the applicant firm ensures this is maintained.

310 "Application for Authorisation – Supplement for firms selling investments – notes" (document, 2021).

Approved persons are approved by the FCA and recorded under the correct controlled functions.
Conflict of interest records are kept.
Financial requirements are maintained.
Notify the FCA immediately of any material breaches of FCA principles/rules.
FCA approval must be granted for changes to: • accounting date; • permitted regulated activities; and • directors and partners.
Adequate management information maintained and provided to senior management.
Documented compliance procedures maintained, used in conjunction with an up-to-date copy of the Handbook.
Anti-money laundering regulations are complied with.

The compliance function's monitoring responsibilities include monitoring "*the actions taken to address any deficiencies*".[311] In practice, a log should be maintained of issues identified during compliance monitoring and follow-up steps taken to remediate them.

311 MiFID Org Regulation art. 22(2)(a).

10.1.3 Compliance Policies and Procedures

Firms must maintain adequate policies and procedures to ensure compliance with their obligations under the regulatory system.[312]

The "**regulatory system**" is defined as (to the extent relevant):

> *[T]he arrangements for regulating a firm or other person in or under [FSMA], including the threshold conditions, Principles for Businesses and other rules, Statements of Principle, codes and guidance, or in or under the CCA, and including any relevant provisions of an onshored regulation such as those contained in the MiFID Org Regulation...*

For investment firms, MiFID Org Regulation art. 22(1) requires proportionate policies and procedures to be put in place that are designed to:

- detect any risk of failure by the firm to comply with its obligations under UK law on markets in financial instruments, as well as associated risks; and
- minimise such risk and to enable the FCA to exercise its power effectively under UK law on markets in financial instruments.

Compliance policies and procedures are likely to be documented in a compliance manual, which a firm may have had to prepare as part of its initial authorisation application to the FCA. Naturally, a firm's compliance policies and procedures should be tailored to that specific firm, although certain topics are mandated by law and regulation or could found an "adequate steps" defence to criminal charges. Some key topics are summarised in the following table:

312 SYSC 6.1.1R.

Topic	Section in this book	Legislative ref.
Diversity of the Management Body	§7.1.1	SYSC 4.3A.10R
Remuneration	§7.2.2, §9.3	MiFID Org Regulation art. 27(1); SYSC 19G.2.1R
Personal transactions by employees	§7.2.4	MiFID Org Regulation art. 29(1)
Data protection	§8.1.1	GDPR art. 24(2)
Business continuity	§8.2	MiFID Org Regulation art. 21(3)
Accounting	§9.3	MiFID Org Regulation art. 21(4)
Conflicts of interest	§11.1	MiFID Org Regulation art. 34(1)
Gifts and entertainment	§11.1.1	COBS 2.3A.5R
Client categorisation	§11.2	COBS 3.8.1R
Complaints handling	§11.5	MiFID Org Regulation art. 26(1)
Order execution	§11.5	COBS 11.2A.20R

Order allocation	§11.5.3	MiFID Org Regulation art. 68(1)(c)
Anti money-laundering	§10.2.1	MLR r. 19
Anti-bribery	§10.2.4	Bribery Act 2010 s. 7(2)
Facilitation of tax evasion	§10.2.7	Criminal Finances Act 2017 ss. 45, 46
Risk management	§10.3.2	MiFID Org Regulation art. 23(1)
Regulatory references	§4.5	SYSC 22.8.1R
Supplemental AIFMD-related policies including: risk management; redemption; valuation; due diligence; holding or management of investments a firm invests on its own account	§13.2.1	FUND 3, SYSC 4.1.1BR(1)
Supplemental EMIR-related procedures covering risk management for non-cleared OTC derivatives	§13.1.1	EMIR art. 11

Additionally, by way of guidance, the FCA includes, in its notes to a retail intermediary firm's authorisation application form,[313] a non-exhaustive list of topics that could or should be included in a compliance manual:

313 "Application for Authorisation – Supplement for firms selling investments – notes" (document, 2021).

Compliance procedures	Other subjects
The scope of the applicant firm's business	Claims handling
Client classification	Chinese walls
Complaints handling	General provisions related to distance marketing
Financial crime	Financial promotion
Training and competence	Rules on personal account transactions
Business continuity	Appointed representatives
The fit and proper criteria for approved persons	The Statement of Principles and Code of Practice for Approved Persons
Communication with clients	Systems and controls in relation to financial crime and money laundering
Record keeping[314]	The employees' responsibilities under the money laundering regime, including: • internal reporting duties; • customer identification procedures; • the use and availability of the know your business information

[314] Of interest may be the FCA internal policy documents "Records Management Principles" and "Retention Schedule" (both publicly available but of unspecified date).

Notifications to the FCA	Client assets
Reporting requirements	
Scope of service provided	
Conflicts of interest	
Remuneration policies	
Exclusion of liability	

10.1.4 Staff Compliance Training

The compliance function is expected to be involved in providing relevant training to a firm's business units. ESMA guidance states that "*[t]raining and other support should focus particularly, but not exclusively, on:*

> *(a) the internal policies and procedures of the firm and its organisational structure in the area of investment services and activities; and*
>
> *(b) MiFID II, its delegated and implementing acts, national implementing laws, the applicable standards, guidelines and other guidance set out by ESMA and competent authorities, any other supervisory and regulatory requirements that may be relevant and any changes to those.*"[315]

In addition, certain topics are mandated for compliance training by specific regulatory provisions, including:

- conduct rules (FSMA s. 64B; COCON 2.3.1G);

[315] "Final report – Guidelines on certain aspects of the MiFID compliance function requirements" (ESMA35-36-1946) (ESMA, 2020).

- money laundering and terrorist financing (MLR r. 24); and
- data protection (GDPR art. 24 – for firms required to appoint a data protection officer).

10.1.5 Compliance Management Information and Reporting

A firm's compliance function should note its obligation "*to report to the management body, on at least an annual basis, on the implementation and effectiveness of the overall control environment for investment services and activities, on the risks that have been identified and on the complaints-handling reporting as well as remedies undertaken or to be undertaken*".[316]

The principal *ad hoc* obligation formally laid on the compliance function is to report "*directly to the management body where it detects a significant risk of failure by the firm to comply with its UK obligations*".[317]

10.2 Financial Crime Risk Oversight

Firms must maintain adequate policies and procedures for countering the risk that they might be used to further financial crime.[318]

"**Financial crime**" is defined as including "*any kind of criminal conduct relating to money or to financial services or markets, including any offence involving: (a) fraud or dishonesty; or (b) misconduct in, or misuse of information relating to, a financial market; or (c) handling the proceeds of crime; or (d) the financing of terrorism*".[319] However, firms should bear in mind that in practice the FCA's jurisdiction is not unduly trammelled by the semantics of technical terminology, with the binding rule in Principle

316 MiFID Org Regulation art. 22(2)(c).

317 MiFID Org Regulation art. 22(3)(c).

318 SYSC 6.1.1R.

319 FSMA s. 1H, which further stipulates that "**offence**" "*includes an act or omission which would be an offence if it had taken place in the United Kingdom*".

1 requiring fundamentally that "*A firm must conduct its business with integrity*".

The FCA's guidance on the steps that a firm can take to reduce the risk that it might be used to further financial crime is located in FCG. FCG 2 covers a firm's financial crime systems and controls, and FCG 3 to 8 deal with various specific types of financial crime in turn, as outlined below. There is also a compendium of FCA financial crime thematic reviews collected at FCTR.[320]

One of the themes set out in FCG 2 is the importance of conducting a financial crime risk assessment.[321] Regarding specific types of financial crime, firms should additionally bear in mind the statutory requirements to conduct assessments for money laundering and terrorist financing risk,[322] and to assess their controls for detecting and reporting potential market abuse.[323] Conducting relevant risk assessments could also form the basis of statutory "adequate procedures" defences to the corporate criminal offences of failure to prevent bribery and failure to prevent the facilitation of tax evasion.

When designing and implementing financial crime compliance systems and controls, firms may wish to refer to the Wolfsberg Group's Correspondent Banking Due Diligence Questionnaire and Financial Crime Compliance Questionnaire, which are used by many financial institutions to gain comfort on prospective clients and counterparties.

---

320 FCG 1.1.5 clarifies that "*[t]he material in FCG does not form part of the Handbook, but it does contain guidance on Handbook rules and principles...*". FCG 1.1.7 adds that "*FCG contains 'general guidance' as defined in section 139B of the Financial Services and Markets Act 2000 (FSMA). The guidance is not binding and we will not presume that a firm's departure from our guidance indicates that it has breached our rules*". FCTR has a similar status (FCTR 1.1.2G).

321 FCG 2.2.4.

322 MLR r. 18(1).

323 MA Reg RTS art. 2(5)(b).

10.2.1 Money Laundering and Terrorist Financing (FCG 3)

"**Money laundering**" is defined as "*any act which: (a) constitutes an offence under section 18 (Money laundering) of the Terrorism Act 2000; or (b) constitutes an offence under section 327 (Concealing etc), section 328 (Arrangements) or section 329 (Acquisition, use and possession) of the Proceeds of Crime Act 2002; or (c) constitutes an attempt, conspiracy or incitement to commit an offence specified in paragraph (b); or (d) constitutes aiding, abetting, counselling or procuring the commission of an offence specified in paragraph (b); or (e) would constitute an offence specified in paragraph (b), (c), or (d) if done in the United Kingdom*".

A firm's regulatory obligations to have systems and controls for countering money laundering risk are spelled out in SYSC 6.3. These include a requirement to appoint an individual as money laundering reporting officer,[324] who will usually thereby be performing a designated senior management function (namely, the money laundering reporting function) which requires FCA approval (see §4.3.2).

In addition, firms must allocate to a director or senior manager overall responsibility for the establishment and maintenance of effective anti-money laundering systems and controls,[325] and should appoint an individual as "**nominated officer**" for the purposes of receiving internal disclosures from staff and submitting corresponding disclosures to the National Crime Agency under the Proceeds of Crime Act 2002 ss. 330 and 331 and Terrorism Act 2000 s. 21A.[326] The nominated officer role

---

324 SYSC 6.3.9R.

325 SYSC 6.3.8R.

326 Such disclosures must be made where the firm's staff member knows or suspects, or has reasonable grounds for knowing or suspecting, that another person is engaged in money laundering or terrorist financing. The test for "**suspecting**" is a relatively low hurdle, and is essentially that the individual "*must think that there is a possibility, which is more than fanciful, that the relevant facts exist*" (*R v Da Silva* [2006] EWCA Crim 1654, in the context of the Criminal Justice Act 1988; confirmed in the context of the Proceeds of Crime Act 2002 in *K Ltd. v National Westminster Bank PLC & Anor.* [2006] EWCA Civ 1185).

may be performed by the same individual as the money laundering reporting function.

Other key planks of a firm's anti money-laundering obligations are:

- applying initial and periodic due diligence measures on customers in the circumstances and manner prescribed in the MLR ss. 27 to 38; and

- conducting money laundering and terrorist financing risk assessments, maintaining proportionate written policies, controls and procedures that cover due diligence and other prescribed topics, and providing appropriate training for staff.[327]

Firms should have regard to the formal industry guidance in this area issued by the Joint Money Laundering Steering Group ("**JMLSG**"),[328] compliance or non-compliance with which is a relevant matter for courts and the FCA in the event of criminal proceedings or enforcement action.[329]

10.2.2 Fraud (FCG 4)

The meaning of "**fraud**" under the Fraud Act 2006 includes various acts of dishonesty (including making false representations, failing to disclose information or abusing a position) which are intended by the offender to make a gain for himself or another, or cause loss to another, as well as secondary offences including possessing, making or supplying articles for fraudulent use, participating in a fraudulent business and obtaining services dishonestly.

---

327 MLR rr. 18-19, 24.

328 "Prevention of money laundering/ combating terrorist financing – guidance for the UK financial sector" (JMLSG, 2017).

329 SYSC 6.3.5G; MLR rr. 19(5), 76(6), 86(2); POCA ss. 330(8), 331(7).

FCA guidance in FCG 4 recognises that firms have strong commercial incentives to protect themselves and their customers from fraud, and focuses on self-assessment questions designed to enable firms to evaluate the full implications of the breadth of fraud risks that they face.

10.2.3 Data Security (FCG 5)

The FCA recommends that firms "*be alert to the financial crime risks associated with holding customer data and have written data security policies and procedures which are proportionate, accurate, up to date and relevant to the day-to-day work of staff*",[330] and provides specific examples of good and bad practice and expected systems and controls.

FCG 5.1.2 cross refers to data protection guidance issued by the ICO.

10.2.4 Bribery and Corruption (FCG 6)

"**Bribery**" comprises three criminal offences under the Bribery Act 2010: (1) offering, promising or giving a financial or other advantage to another person in connection with that person performing a function improperly; (2) requesting, agreeing to receive or accepting a financial or other advantage from another person in connection with that person performing a function improperly; and (3) offering, promising or giving a financial or other advantage to a foreign public official with the intention of influencing him in his capacity as a foreign public official, in order to obtain or retain business or an advantage in the conduct of business.[331]

The Bribery Act 2010 also creates a strict-liability corporate offence of "**failure to prevent bribery**", where a commercial organisation fails to

---

330 FCG 5.2.1

331 Bribery Act 2010 ss. 1-2, 6.

prevent an associated person[332] from bribing another person with the intent to obtain or retain business or an advantage in the conduct of business.[333] There is a defence if the commercial organisation can prove that it had in place adequate procedures designed to prevent associated persons from undertaking such conduct. In designing such "adequate procedures", firms may wish to consult the guidance issued by the Ministry of Justice which incorporates six principles including risk assessment and communication of procedures.[334]

10.2.5 Sanctions and Asset Freezes (FCG 7)

Financial sanctions are restrictions put in place to achieve a specific foreign policy or national security objective.[335] In the UK, they may be imposed at the initiative of either the UK Government or the UN, and the most common types are:

- targeted asset freezes, which restrict named individuals' and entities' access to funds and economic resources;

---

332 "**Associated person**" is defined as (essentially) any "person who performs services for or on behalf of" the commercial organisation (Bribery Act 2010 s. 8), and typically would include directors, employees, interns, consultants, temporary workers, third-party service providers and other agents.

333 Bribery Act 2010 s. 7.

334 "The Bribery Act 2010 – Guidance about procedures which relevant commercial organisations can put into place to prevent persons associated with them from bribing (section 9 of the Bribery Act 2010)" (Ministry of Justice, 2011).

335 "UK Financial Sanctions – General guidance for financial sanctions under the Sanctions and Anti-Money Laundering Act 2018" (HM Treasury/OFSI, 2020).

- restrictions on a wide variety of financial markets and services, which can apply to named individuals and entities, specified groups, or entire sectors;[336] and
- directions to cease all business of a specified type with a specific person, group, sector or country.

Formally, financial sanctions are implemented in the UK through a combination of statutory instruments[337] and primary legislation[338] which make it a criminal offence to breach the financial sanction in question.

A consolidated list of persons and organisations subject to UK financial sanctions is published by HM Treasury's Office for Financial Sanctions Implementation ("**OFSI**").

10.2.6 Insider Dealing and Market Manipulation (FCG 8)

Criminal offences relating to insider dealing and market manipulation are defined in the Criminal Justice Act 1993 s. 52 and Financial Services Act 2012 ss. 89 to 91.

There is also a civil regime under the MA Reg which creates an analogous set of regulatory offences of insider dealing[339] and market

---

336 To date these have taken the form of: investment bans; restrictions on access to capital markets; directions to cease banking relationships and activities; requirements to notify or seek authorisation prior to certain payments being made or received; and/or restrictions on the provision of financial, insurance, brokering or advisory services or other financial services.

337 Including the Global Human Rights Sanctions Regulations 2020 and Global Anti-Corruption Sanctions Regulations 2021.

338 Principally, the Sanctions and Anti-Money Laundering Act 2018, Counter Terrorism Act 2008 and Anti-Terrorism, Crime and Security Act 2001.

339 MA Reg arts. 7 to 11.

manipulation[340] (collectively, "**market abuse**"). Detailed descriptions of behaviours amounting to market abuse, and an overview of statutory exceptions, are set out in MAR.[341]

Technically, FCA guidance in FCG 8 covers only the criminal and not the regulatory offences. However, the FCA does suggest that firms may find it simpler to consider the guidance as applying to all instruments to which both regimes apply.[342]

In addition to FCG 8, useful FCA resources on practices and procedures to control the risk of market abuse include the Market Watch newsletters and "Asset management firms and the risk of market abuse" (TR15/1), which has not yet been included in FCTR. Firms are also reminded that, under SYSC 10.2, having Chinese walls in place can provide a defence to criminal and regulatory insider dealing offences (see §8.1.3).

Firms that arrange or execute transactions are under specific obligations to have systems that ensure effective monitoring to detect potential market abuse (and attempts),[343] to enable "*analysis, individually and comparatively, of each and every transaction executed and order placed, modified, cancelled or rejected*", and to *"produce alerts indicating activities*

---

340 MA Reg art. 12 and Annex I. Supplemented by MA Reg Delegated Regulation, "Questions and Answers On the Market Abuse Regulation (MAR)" (ESMA70-145-111) (ESMA, 2021), "MAR Guidelines: Information relating to commodity derivatives markets or related spot markets for the purpose of the definition of inside information on commodity derivatives" (ESMA/2016/1480) (ESMA, 2017), and "Final Report – Draft technical standards on the Market Abuse Regulation" (ESMA/2015/1455) (ESMA, 2015).

341 The FCA also issues standalone items on its "Market abuse" webpage, such as its expectations for firms that handle information obtained via electoral polling (see "Polling and Market Abuse Regulation" (webpage, 2021)). Elsewhere, other formally-recognised resources examining the parameters of market abusive behaviour include FX Global Code (Global Foreign Exchange Committee, 2021) and Global Precious Metals Code (London Bullion Market Association, 2017).

342 FCG 8.1.5.

343 MA Reg RTS art. 2(1).

requiring further analysis".[344] Suspicious transactions and orders must be notified to the FCA (see §5.3).

Finally, firms should bear in mind Principle 5, which states: "*A firm must observe proper standards of market conduct.*" This rule can enable the FCA, in enforcement proceedings, to curtail technical arguments over the strict legal definitions of "insider dealing" and "market manipulation".

10.2.7 Failure to Prevent the Facilitation of Tax Evasion

One type of criminal conduct not currently addressed in FCG is the strict-liability corporate offence of "**failure to prevent the facilitation of tax evasion**" created by the Criminal Finances Act 2017, which is committed by a corporate or partnership that fails to prevent an associated person[345] from committing a UK or foreign tax evasion facilitation offence.[346]

As with the corporate offence of failure to prevent bribery, there is a defence if the commercial organisation can prove that it had in place adequate procedures designed to prevent associated persons from undertaking such conduct. In designing such "adequate procedures", firms may wish to consult the guidance issued by HMRC which incorporates six principles including risk assessment and communication

---

344 MA Reg RTS art. 3(1).

345 "**Associated persons**" comprise any "*person who performs services for or on behalf of*" the corporate (Criminal Finances Act 2017 s. 44), and typically would include directors, employees, interns, consultants, temporary workers, third-party service providers and other agents.

346 Criminal Finances Act 2017 ss. 45, 46.

of procedures.[347] Regard may also be had to the formal industry guidance issued by UK Finance.[348]

10.3 Risk Control

Principle 3 states: "*A firm must take reasonable care to organise and control its affairs responsibly and effectively, with adequate risk management systems.*" This rule is developed in SYSC 4.1.1R(1), which requires firms to have "*effective processes to identify, manage, monitor and report the risks it is or might be exposed to*".

For investment firms, the more detailed "risk management" and "risk management function" requirements of MiFID Org Regulation art. 23 apply. These are supplemented (for MIFIDPRU investment firms) by the risk management provisions in MIFIDPRU 7.

10.3.1 Risk Management

Under MiFID Org Regulation art. 23(1), a firm must:

- establish, implement and maintain adequate risk management policies and procedures which identify the risks relating to the firm's activities, processes and systems, and where appropriate, set the level of risk tolerated by the firm;

- adopt effective arrangements, processes and mechanisms to manage the risks relating to the firm's activities, processes and systems, in light of that level of risk tolerance;

---

347 "Tackling tax evasion: Government guidance for the corporate offences of failure to prevent the criminal facilitation of tax evasion" (HM Revenue & Customs, 2017).

348 "Failure to prevent the criminal facilitation of tax evasion – Guidance for the financial services sector on the corporate criminal offences within the Criminal Finances Act 2017" (UK Finance, 2018).

- monitor the following:
  - the adequacy and effectiveness of its risk management policies and procedures;
  - the level of compliance by it and its relevant persons with the risk management arrangements, processes and mechanisms; and
  - the adequacy and effectiveness of measures taken to address any deficiencies in those policies, procedures, arrangements, processes and mechanisms, including failures by the relevant persons to comply with such arrangements, processes and mechanisms or follow such policies and procedures.[349]

SYSC 7.1 includes supplemental rules and guidance on risk assessment and risk management. Notably, a firm's management body must approve and periodically review the strategies and policies for taking up, managing, monitoring and mitigating the risks that the firm is or might be exposed to, including those posed by the macroeconomic environment in which it operates in relation to the status of the business cycle.[350]

Further supplemental risk management provisions exist for a MIFIDPRU investment firm, whose management body is charged with overall responsibility for risk management and must:

- devote sufficient time to the consideration of risk;

---

349 MiFID Org Regulation art. 23(1).

350 SYSC 7.1.4R. This would include reverse stress testing, if the firm had assets under management/administration of at least £10 billion; or the total annual fee and commission arising from regulated activities were at least £250 million; or it had assets or liabilities of at least £2 billion (SYSC 20.1.1A(2)).

- be actively involved in, and ensure that adequate resources are allocated to, the management of all material risks, including the valuation of assets, the use of external ratings and internal models relating to those risks; and

- establish reporting lines to the management body that cover all material risks and risk management policies and changes thereof.[351]

Further, the management body and any risk committee that has been established[352] must have adequate access to information on the risk profile of the firm and, if necessary and appropriate, to the risk management function and to external expert advice, and must determine the nature, the amount, the format, and the frequency of the information on risk which they are to receive.[353]

10.3.2 Risk Management Function

Under MiFID Org Regulation art. 23(2), a firm must, where appropriate and proportionate in view of the nature, scale and complexity of their business and the nature and range of the investment services and activities undertaken in the course of that business, establish and maintain a risk management function that operates independently and carries out the following tasks:

- implementation of the risk management policy and procedures; and

- provision of reports (at least annually) to senior management.

---

351 MIFIDPRU 7.2.3R.

352 Under MIFIDPRU 7.3.1R, non-SNI MIFIDPRU investment firms which exceed prescribed quantitative ceilings (see §7.1.3) must establish a risk committee.

353 MIFIDPRU 7.2.4R.

Firms are reminded in SYSC 7.1 to consider the additional guidance on risk-centric governance arrangements for effective risk management contained in SYSC 21,[354] and to comply with any relevant remuneration code in setting the method of determining the remuneration of employees involved in the risk management function.[355]

Additionally, a non-SNI MIFIDPRU investment firm that has a risk management function in accordance with MIFID Org Regulation art. 23 must ensure that its risk management function is independent from its operational functions and has sufficient authority, stature, resources and access to the management body.[356] The head of the risk management function must be an independent senior manager with distinct responsibility for the risk management function, unless this is not justified by the nature, scale and complexity of the activities of the firm (in which case another senior person within the firm may fulfil that function, provided there is no conflict of interest).[357]

10.4 Internal Audit

Under MiFID Org Regulation art. 24, a firm must – where appropriate and proportionate in view of the nature, scale and complexity of its business and the nature and range of its investment services and activities – establish and maintain an appropriate internal audit function which is separate and independent from the other functions and activities of the firm and which has certain prescribed responsibilities.[358]

---

354 SYSC 7.1.7CG.

355 SYSC 7.1.7BG to 7BDG.

356 MIFIDPRU 7.2A.2R.

357 MIFIDPRU 7.2A.3R.

358 Namely: (1) to establish, implement and maintain an audit plan to examine and evaluate the adequacy and effectiveness of the firm's systems, internal control mechanisms and arrangements; (2) to issue recommendations based on the result

Responsibility for overseeing the functioning of any internal audit function could sit with an audit committee established pursuant to FCA guidance at SYSC 4.1.11G.

---

of work carried out in accordance with (1); (3) to verify compliance with those recommendations; and (4) to provide appropriate management information in relation to internal audit matters.

PART C

CONDUCT OF BUSINESS

11 TREATING CUSTOMERS FAIRLY

Principle 6 states: "*A firm must pay due regard to the interests of its customers and treat them fairly.*"

This precept is further developed in Principles 7 ("Clients' information needs" – see §11.4), 8 ("Conflicts of interest" – see §11.1) and 9 ("Suitability of advice and discretionary decisions" – see §11.3).

Rules governing how firms treat and communicate with their clients are located primarily in COBS, bolstered by guidance in UNFCOG[359] and RPPD.[360] Special regimes also exist for certain business including AIFMs (see §13.2) and consumer credit (see §13.3).

In some situations, a preliminary question may arise as to who a firm's client is. COBS 2.4.3R provides that, if a firm is aware that its direct client has, in turn, an underlying client, generally the direct client (and not the underlying client) will remain the firm's client. This is the case unless either (a) the firm has agreed otherwise in writing, or (b) the direct client is not an investment firm and the arrangements are designed to avoid the duties that the firm would otherwise owe to the underlying client.

In addition to the regulatory framework outlined below, redress through a civil claim may be available to aggrieved clients who believe that a firm has not treated them fairly. For example, FSMA s. 138D(2) provides that

---

359 Made under Consumer Rights Act 2015 (see UNFCOG 1.2.3G(4)). UNFCOG "*explains the FCA's policy on how it will use its powers under the Consumer Rights Act 2015 in relation to unfair terms and consumer notices*" (UNFCOG 1.1.1G).

360 Issued as non-binding guidance under FSMA s. 139A (see RPPD 1.3). The purpose of RPPD is to "*give [the FCA's] view on what the combination of [Principles] and detailed rules require respectively of providers and distributors in certain circumstances to treat customers fairly*" (RPPD 1.1).

"*[a] contravention by an authorised person of a rule made by the FCA is actionable at the suit of a private person who suffers loss as a result of the contravention, subject to the defences and other incidents applying to actions for breach of statutory duty*". Separately, there may be criminal liability where (most notably) a firm's conduct has involved dishonesty. Such non-regulatory processes are beyond the scope of this book.

11.1 Conflicts of Interest

Investment firms must comply with the requirements pertaining to conflicts of interest set out in MiFID Org Regulation arts. 33 to 35 and selected provisions of SYSC 10.1.

A "**conflict of interest**" is defined in MiFID Org Regulation art. 33 essentially as follows:

> *For the purposes of identifying types of conflicts of interest... investment firms shall take into account, by way of minimum criteria, whether the investment firm or a relevant person, or a person directly or indirectly linked by control to the firm, is in any of the following situations...:*
>
> *(a) the firm or that person is likely to make a financial gain, or avoid a financial loss, at the expense of the client;*
>
> *(b) the firm or that person has an interest in the outcome of a service provided to the client or of a transaction carried out on behalf of the client, which is distinct from the client's interest in that outcome;*
>
> *(c) the firm or that person has a financial or other incentive to favour the interest of another client or group of clients over the interests of the client;*
>
> *(d) the firm or that person carries on the same business as the client;*
>
> *(e) the firm or that person receives or will receive from a person other than the client an inducement in relation to a service*

> *provided to the client, in the form of monetary or non-monetary benefits or services.*

As a general matter, firms must:

- identify and prevent or manage conflicts of interest between: (1) the firm, including its managers, employees and appointed representatives (or where applicable, tied agents), or any person directly or indirectly linked to them by control, and a client of the firm; or (2) one client of the firm and another client;[361]

- maintain and operate effective organisational and administrative arrangements with a view to taking all reasonable steps to prevent such conflicts of interest;[362]

- as a last resort, where such arrangements are not sufficient to ensure with reasonable confidence that risks of damage to the interests of a client will be prevented, clearly disclose to a client before undertaking business: (1) the general nature or sources of conflicts of interest, or both; and (2) the steps taken to mitigate those risks;[363]

- establish, implement and maintain an effective conflicts of interest policy set out in writing and appropriate to the size and organisation of the firm and the nature, scale and complexity of its business, with the content prescribed in MiFID Org Regulation art.34(2) and (3) and considering the guidance at SYSC 10.1.12G;[364]

---

361 SYSC 10.1.3R.

362 SYSC 10.1.7R.

363 SYSC 10.1.8R; MiFID Org Regulation art. 34(4).

364 MiFID Org Regulation art. 34(1).

- assess and periodically review, at least annually, the conflicts of interest policy;[365]
- keep and regularly update a record of the kinds of investment or ancillary service or investment activity carried out by or on behalf of the firm in which a conflict of interest entailing a risk of damage to the interests of one or more clients has arisen or, in the case of an ongoing service or activity, may arise;[366] and
- ensure that senior management receive on a frequent basis, and at least annually, written reports on situations in which a conflict of interest entailing a risk of damage to the interests of one or more clients has arisen or, in the case of an ongoing service or activity, may arise.[367]

11.1.1 Inducements and Receiving Research

As one means of preventing actual or potential conflicts of interest, a firm must not pay or accept any fee, commission or non-monetary benefit (collectively referred to informally as "**inducements**" in the FCA Handbook and MiFID Org Regulation) to or from a third party in connection with its investment business.[368]

This prohibition does not apply to:

- an inducement which:

---

365 MiFID Org Regulation art. 34(5). Of some illustrative value are the FCA's own policy ("The Financial Conduct Authority – Conflict of Interests Policy" (document, 2019)) and ESMA's own policy ("Conflict of interests and ethics – Policy – ESMA Staff" (ESMA40-134-2458) (ESMA, 2020) – including "Template 3 – Annual declaration of interests" which ESMA publishes in relation to certain senior staff).

366 MiFID Org Regulation art. 35 para. 1.

367 MiFID Org Regulation art. 35 para. 2.

368 COBS 2.3A.5R.

- is "*designed to enhance the quality of the relevant service to the client*";[369] and

- does not impair compliance with the firm's duty to act honestly, fairly and professionally in the best interests of the client,

  in which case, such inducement must be disclosed to the client in accordance with COBS 2.3A.6R(2)-(4);

➢ a payment or benefit which enables or is necessary for the provision of an investment service by the firm, such as custody costs, settlement and exchange fees, regulatory levies or legal fees and which, by its nature, cannot give rise to conflicts with the firm's duty to act honestly, fairly and professionally in the best interests of the client; or

➢ third-party research[370] that is not an inducement by virtue of having been received in return for either:

- direct payments by the firm out of its own resources; or

---

[369] As defined in COBS 2.3A.8R.

[370] "**Research**" for these purposes is defined as "*research material or services: concerning one or several financial instruments or other assets; or concerning the issuers or potential issuers of financial instruments; or closely related to a specific industry or market such that it informs views on financial instruments, assets or issuers within that sector, and which explicitly or implicitly recommends or suggests an investment strategy and provides a substantiated opinion as to the present or future value or price of such instruments or assets, or otherwise contains analysis and original insights and reaches conclusions based on new or existing information that could be used to inform an investment strategy or be capable of adding value to a firm's decisions on behalf of clients*".

- payments from a separate research payment account controlled by the firm that complies with COBS 2.3B.4R.[371]

The price of third-party research should be properly assessed by the firm, either to avoid being so undervalued as to constitute an inducement (if paid for out of the firm's own resources), or to comply with the assessment and budgeting requirements in COBS 2.3B (if paid for using a research payment account).

For inducements received in relation to the provision of independent advice, restricted advice or portfolio management services, COBS 2.3A.15R, 16R and 19R contain supplemental restrictions as well as concomitant carve-outs for (notably) benefits which are deemed to be "**acceptable minor non-monetary benefits**".

Certain types of third-party research received by firms may constitute an acceptable minor-non-monetary benefit and, if so, it does not require payment to comply with the inducement rules. This includes research received for evaluation purposes during a free trial period lasting no longer than three months,[372] as well as "*macro-economic-related material [made] openly available at the same time to any investment firms or to the general public on a website*" and certain other types of research described in ESMA guidance.[373] "FCA statement on MiFID II inducements and research" (webpage, 2017) also makes allowances for arrangements where a UK asset manager pays the EU entity of a broker for global research content, or where research is circulated within a buy-side group, and notes that the U.S. Securities and Exchange Commission has issued no-

---

371 COBS 2.3A.6R, 3B.3R. Firms should take reasonable steps to cease receiving (or avoid benefiting from) "free" research material that it does not want to accept and pay for, such as setting up email filters: see "Questions and Answers On MiFID II and MiFIR investor protection and intermediaries topics" (ESMA35-43-349) (ESMA, 2021), Chapter 7 Q.3.

372 COBS 2.3A.19R(5)(f).

373 "Questions and Answers on MiFID II and MiFIR investor protection and intermediaries topics" (ESMA35-43-349) (ESMA, 2021).

action letters which enable U.S. broker-dealers to charge for investment research for the time being.[374]

Where investment research does not constitute an acceptable minor non-monetary benefit, it must be paid for in order to comply with the rules against inducements. Firms should note that "*the 'black letter law' on inducements does not differentiate between whether a research supplier is a broker – where a conflict of interest can clearly arise – or an independent provider*". However, the FCA has indicated that "*independent providers can pitch for business and offer sample material on an ad-hoc basis without it being an inducement for an asset manager*".[375]

11.1.2 Communicating Investment Recommendations and Investment Research

Firms that produce or disseminate investment recommendations must "*take reasonable care to ensure that such information is objectively presented, and to disclose their interests or indicate conflicts of interest concerning the financial instruments to which that information relates*".[376]

An "**investment recommendation**" is defined in MA Reg art. 3(1)(35) as:

---

374 From March 2022, the list of acceptable minor non-monetary benefits in COBS 2.3A.19R will be extended to include research on small and mid-cap listed or unlisted companies (SMEs) who have a market capitalisation below £200m, and third-party research on fixed income currencies and commodities instruments (but not macro-economic research). Also exempt will be research providers who do not provide execution services and are not part of a group that includes a firm offering execution services, and it will be formally clarified that openly available written research is similarly out of scope.

375 A. Bailey, "Keynote speech on MiFID II" (speech, European Independent Research Providers Association, London, 25/02/2019).

376 MA Reg art. 20(1). See also COBS 12.4.

> *information recommending or suggesting an investment strategy,*[377] *explicitly or implicitly, concerning one or several financial instruments or the issuers, including any opinion as to the present or future value or price of such instruments, intended for distribution channels or for the public.*

The FCA regards investment recommendations as comprising two sub-categories:[378]

- "**investment research**", which is defined as "*research or other information recommending or suggesting an investment strategy, explicitly or implicitly, concerning one or several financial instruments or the issuers of financial instruments, including any opinion as to the present or future value or price of such instruments, intended for distribution channels or for the public, and in relation to which the following conditions are met:*

  (a) the research or information is labelled or described as investment research or in similar terms, or is otherwise presented as an objective or independent explanation of the matters contained in the recommendation;

  (b) if the recommendation in question were made by an investment firm to a client, it would not constitute the

---

377 "**Information recommending or suggesting an investment strategy**" means, in turn: "*information: (i) produced by an independent analyst, an investment firm, a credit institution, any other person whose main business is to produce investment recommendations or a natural person working for them under a contract of employment or otherwise, which, directly or indirectly, expresses a particular investment proposal in respect of a financial instrument or an issuer; or (ii) produced by persons other than those referred to in point (i), which directly proposes a particular investment decision in respect of a financial instrument*" (MA Reg art. 3(1)(34)).

378 COBS 12.2.16G.

provision of investment advice for the purposes of UK law on markets in financial instruments";[379] and

- "**non-independent research**", which is (in summary) an investment recommendation that does not meet the conditions for investment research.[380]

Firms producing or arranging for the production of investment research or non-independent research must implement an appropriate conflicts of interest policy that covers their "*financial analysts involved in the production of the investment research and other relevant persons whose responsibilities or business interests may conflict with the interests of the persons to whom the investment research is disseminated*".[381]

In relation specifically to investment research, firms must have in place arrangements designed to ensure that the conditions listed in MiFID Org Regulation art. 37(2) are satisfied.[382]

Non-independent research is treated as marketing communication, and must both be clearly identified as such and contain "*a clear and prominent statement that (or, in the case of an oral recommendation, to the effect that) it has not been prepared in accordance with legal requirements designed to promote the independence of investment research, and that it is not subject to any prohibition on dealing ahead of the dissemination of investment research*".[383]

---

379 FCA Handbook Glossary, with reference to MiFID Org Regulation art. 36(1). Investment advice is considered in §11.1.3.

380 FCA Handbook Glossary, naming a concept which is described in MiFID Org Regulation art. 36(2).

381 MiFID Org Regulation art. 37(1). See also COBS 12.2.19UK.

382 See also COBS 12.2.21UK. Certain exemptions apply for firms disseminating third-party investment research (see MiFID Org Regulation art. 37(3) and COBS 12.2.22UK).

383 MiFID Org Regulation art. 36(2). See also COBS 12.2.18UK.

11.1.3 Investment Advice

MiFID Org Regulation arts. 52 and 53 govern the provision of investment advice. Their requirements are reproduced in COBS 6.2B, which also extends the scope to certain non-MiFID retail business in the UK.

"**Investment advice**" is defined as "*the provision of personal recommendations to a client, either upon the client's request or at the initiative of the firm, in respect of one or more transactions relating to designated investments*".

Investment advice may be provided on either an "independent" or a "non-independent" (also referred to as "**restricted**")[384] basis.

"**Independent advice**" is defined as "*a personal recommendation to a client where the personal recommendation provided meets the requirements of the rule on independent advice (COBS 6.2B.11R)*". In this context, a "**personal recommendation**" is:

> *a recommendation:*
>
> *(a) made to a person in their capacity as an investor or potential investor, or in their capacity as agent for an investor or a potential investor;*
>
> *(b) which constitutes a recommendation to them to do any of the following (whether as principal or agent):*
>
> *(i) buy, sell, subscribe for, exchange, redeem, hold or underwrite a particular investment which is a security, a structured deposit or a relevant investment (that is, any designated investment (other than a P2P agreement), funeral plan contract, pure protection contract, general*

[384] COBS 6.2B.10G.

insurance contract, right to or interests in a funeral plan contract or structured deposit); or

(ii) *exercise or not exercise any right conferred by such a relevant investment to buy, sell, subscribe for, exchange or redeem such an investment;*

(c) *that is:*

(i) *presented as suitable for the person to whom it is made; or*

(ii) *based on a consideration of the circumstances of that person; and*

(d) *that is not issued exclusively to the public.*

The "**rule on independent advice**" in COBS 6.2B.11R is, in summary, that the firm must assess a sufficient range of relevant products available on the market that is (1) sufficiently diverse to ensure that the client's investment objectives can be suitably met, and (2) not limited to relevant products issued or provided by (a) the firm itself or by entities having close links with the firm, or (b) other entities with which the firm has close legal or economic relationships.

Firms must give certain prescribed information to clients about the "independent" or "non-independent" status of the investment advice provided.[385]

A firm that provides independent advice must comply with detailed requirements on the selection of financial instruments, presentation of information and separation of staff functions.[386]

---

385 MiFID Org Regulation art. 52. See also COBS 6.2B.32UK to 39G.

386 MiFID Org Regulation art. 53. See also COBS 6.2B.14G to 31G.

11.1.4 Underwriting and Placing

Additional requirements aimed at mitigating the risk of conflicts of interest in the context of providing underwriting and placing services are set out in MiFID Org Regulation arts. 38 to 43. These are reproduced and supplemented in COBS 11A.1.

11.1.5 Payment for Order Flow

One type of conflict of interest which can arise in the wholesale markets and which has been a focus of the FCA in recent years is the practice of "payment for order flow" ("**PFOF**"), whereby a broker executing an order for a client receives a fee or commission from both the client and the liquidity provider.

The FCA considers that such payments "*create a conflict of interest... because they incentivise the firm to execute its clients' orders with counterparties based on their willingness to pay commissions... PFOF makes it more likely that extra costs will be passed on to the broker's client, through wider bid-ask spreads from market makers and other liquidity providers who agree to pay PFOF to attract order flow from brokers*". PFOF also "*risks inferior execution outcomes*", thus potentially compromising firms' compliance with best execution obligations (see §11.5.1).[387]

The FCA recognises two main scenarios in which brokers may receive PFOF: (i) where the broker is sourcing exclusive liquidity for a specific client – in which case it should not accept PFOF; and (ii) where the broker is broadly disseminating non-exclusive liquidity, for example through electronic channels or call-arounds – in which case PFOF may be tolerable.

Where, in the second scenario, a broker does accept PFOF, the FCA's view is that the broker should comply with the conflicts of interest rules by:

---

[387] "Payment for Order Flow (PFOF)" (document, 2019).

- identifying in its written conflicts of interest policy the potential conflicts from double-sided charges and the steps taken to manage those conflicts;
- codifying procedures for order handling, execution and allocations, which must be effective in preventing the risk of harm to clients;
- considering how it explains to clients how it acts when sourcing exclusive or non-exclusive liquidity, and how it handles trading interests and allocates orders according;
- limiting the range of, or harmonising, charges for some or all clients, thus removing the financial incentive to favour one client over another due to different fee levels;
- monitoring transactions to check that, when the broker's capacity has been explicitly or effectively to source exclusive liquidity, PFOF has not been received.

11.1.6 Other Controls against Conflicts of Interest

Other regulatory requirements that are relevant to a firm's mitigation of conflicts of interest include those relating to: remuneration (see §7.2.2 and §9.3); personal account dealing (see §7.2.4); and Chinese walls (§8.1.3).

11.2 Client Categorisation

All clients of a firm fall within one of three categories: retail client, professional client or eligible counterparty. In summary, each of these has the following characteristics:

"Retail clients" (summary)
By default, any client that is not a professional client or eligible counterparty is categorised as a "**retail client**". In principle, retail clients enjoy the highest level of client protections available under the regulatory system.
"Professional clients" (summary)
"**Professional clients**" comprise regulated firms, large undertakings and other types of entity as specified in COBS 3.5.2R ("**per se professional clients**"), as well as other clients whom a firm has formally opted up to "professional client" status following the procedure set out in COBS 3.5.3R ("**elective professional clients**"). Note that COBS 3.5.2BR clarifies that a local public authority or municipality which (in either case) does not manage public debt must be categorised as a retail client (unless opted up as an elective professional client). Professional clients are entitled to fewer protections than retail clients – most notably, in relation to: • information requirements (MiFID Org Regulation arts. 44(4), 48, 50 = COBS 4.5A.10UK; COBS 6.1ZA.2.7R to 12R; COBS 14.3A.5UK); • order execution policy (MiFID Org Regulation art. 66(9) = COBS 11.2A.25UK(9)); • best execution (MiFID Org Regulation art. 64 = COBS 11.2A); • difficulty in carrying out orders (MiFID Org Regulation art. 67(1) = COBS 11.3.2AUK); • custody (CASS 6.1.6R; CASS 6.2.3(4)R; CASS 6.4.1R to 2G); • client money (CASS 7.11.1R, 32R);

- 10% depreciation reporting (MiFID Org Regulation art. 62(2) = COBS 16A.4.3UK);[388]
- suitability and appropriateness (MiFID Org Regulation arts. 54, 56 = COBS 9A.2.1R, 5UK; COBS 9A.3.2R; COBS 10.2.1R; COBS 10A.2.3UK);
- remuneration incentives (MiFID Org Regulation art. 27 = SYSC 19F.1.4R);
- share trading obligation (MiFIR art. 23); and
- exclusion of liability (COBS 2.1.3G).

"Eligible counterparties" (summary)

"**Eligible counterparties**" are a subset of per se professional clients, and similarly must be either "**per se eligible counterparties**" or "**elective eligible counterparties**" as detailed in COBS 3.6.2R to 6R. A client can only be an eligible counterparty in respect of eligible counterparty business.[389]

Eligible counterparties receive the lowest level of client protections. The COBS rules that are generally disapplied for eligible counterparty business are set out in COBS 1 Annex 1 Part 1, 1.1R, and these include rules relating to: the content and frequency of disclosures, reports, notifications and other communications from the firm; clients' best interests; and the payment and acceptance of inducements.

---

[388] As noted in §11.4.2 and footnote 427, there is currently an exception in the context of portfolio management services where professional clients do enjoy this protection, although regulations have already been made which remove this protection.

[389] "**Eligible counterparty business**" is defined as (essentially): "*(a) dealing on own account, execution of orders on behalf of clients or reception and transmission of orders; or (b) any ancillary service directly related to a service or activity referred to in (a); or (c) arranging in relation to business which is not MiFID or equivalent third country firm business*".

A firm must:

- notify clients of their categorisation as a retail client, professional client or eligible counterparty;[390]

- inform clients in a durable medium about any right that client has to request a different categorisation and about any limitations to the level of client protection that a different categorisation would entail;[391] and

- implement appropriate written internal policies and procedures to categorise its clients.[392]

Where a firm is instructed to provide an investment service for a client through a third-party investment firm, the firm is entitled to rely upon information about the client that it receives from that investment firm. The third-party investment firm will remain responsible for the completeness and accuracy of such information.[393]

There are no specific ongoing obligations on a firm to actively refresh its categorisation of its clients. FCA guidance makes it clear that professional clients are responsible for keeping a firm informed about any change that could affect their current categorisation.[394]

---

390 MiFID Org Regulation art. 45(1) (= COBS 3.3.1AUK).

391 MiFID Org Regulation art. 45(2) (= COBS 3.3.1AUK). However, a firm need not notify a client of a right to request a different categorisation involving a lower level of protection if it would not be prepared to consider such requests (COBS 3.3.2G).

392 COBS 3.8.1R.

393 COBS 2.4.4R.

394 COBS 3.5.8G.

11.3 Suitability and Appropriateness

11.3.1 Suitability

Principle 9 states: "*A firm must take reasonable care to ensure the suitability of its advice and discretionary decisions for any customer who is entitled to rely upon its judgment.*"

The obligation to ensure the suitability of recommendations and decisions to trade is stated at COBS 9A.2.1R(2), which highlights in particular the client's risk tolerance and ability to bear losses as criteria for determining suitability.

In order to be able to make the suitability assessment, under MiFID Org Regulation art. 54(2)[395] a firm must "*obtain from clients or potential clients such information as is necessary for the firm to understand the essential facts about the client and to have a reasonable basis for determining, giving due consideration to the nature and extent of the service provided, that the specific transaction to be recommended, or entered into in the course of providing a portfolio management service, satisfies the following criteria:*

(a) it meets the investment objectives of the client in question, including client's risk tolerance;[396]

(b) it is such that the client is able financially to bear any related investment risks consistent with his investment objectives;[397] *and*

---

395 = COBS 9A.2.4UK.

396 Must include, where relevant, information on the length of time for which the client wishes to hold the investment, his preferences regarding risk taking, his risk profile, and the purposes of the investment (MiFID Org Regulation art. 54(5) (= COBS 9A.2.8UK)).

397 Can be assumed to be satisfied in the case of per se professional clients (MiFID Org Regulation art. 54(3) (= COBS 9A.2.5UK)).

(c) *it is such that the client has the necessary experience and knowledge in order to understand the risks involved in the transaction or in the management of his portfolio.*"[398]

Where a firm is instructed to provide an investment service for a client through a third-party investment firm, the firm is entitled to rely upon information about the client that it receives from that investment firm as well as any recommendations that have been provided to the client by that investment firm. The third-party investment firm will remain responsible both for the completeness and accuracy of such information and for the suitability of advice or recommendations provided to the client. The firm's responsibility then will be to conclude the services or transaction based on any such information or recommendations in accordance with the applicable requirements under the regulatory system.[399]

Firms that have an ongoing relationship with a client must have appropriate policies and procedures to maintain adequate and up-to-date information about clients to the extent necessary to fulfil the suitability assessment requirements.[400]

Firms may find useful additional material in "Final Report – Guidelines on certain aspects of the MiFID II suitability requirements" (ESMA35-43-869) (ESMA, 2018).

11.3.2 Appropriateness

Where a firm provides investment services other than making a personal recommendation or portfolio management – that is, when providing what is typically described as "non-advised" or "execution-only" services – the firm generally must ask the client to provide sufficient information

---

398 Can be assumed to be satisfied in the case of professional clients (MiFID Org Regulation art. 54(3) (= COBS 9A.2.5UK)).

399 COBS 2.4.4R, 5G.

400 COBS 9A.2.10UK.

about his relevant knowledge and experience to enable the firm to perform an appropriateness assessment.[401]

As an exception, COBS 10A.4.1R provides that an appropriate assessment need not be performed if (in summary):

- the service (1) only consists of execution or reception and transmission of client orders (with or without ancillary services) and excludes the granting of new credits or loans, (2) relates to financial instruments listed at COBS 10A.4.1R(2),[402] and (3) is provided at the initiative of the client;[403]

- the client has been clearly informed that the firm is not required to perform an appropriateness assessment and that therefore the client does not benefit from the protection of the rules on assessing appropriateness; and

- the firm complies with its obligations in relation to conflicts of interest.

Further, a firm need not assess appropriateness if:

- it is receiving or transmitting an order or carrying on insurance distribution in relation to an insurance-based investment product, for which it has assessed suitability under COBS 9A; or

---

401 COBS 10A.1.1R, 2.1R.

402 Namely: certain non-complex types of listed shares, listed bonds, money-market instruments, UCITS, structured deposits, and other "**non-complex financial instruments**" as defined in MiFID Org Regulation art. 57 (= COBS 10A.4.2UK).

403 There is guidance on what may be considered "**client's own initiative**" at COBS 10A.5.

- it is able to rely on a recommendation made by an investment firm as described at COBS 2.4.5G.[404]

Where an appropriateness assessment is required, the firm must determine whether the client has the necessary experience and knowledge in order to understand the relevant risks involved.[405] This can be assumed to be satisfied in the case of clients who are categorised as professional clients in relation to the products or services in question;[406] in all other cases, MiFID Org Regulation art. 55(1)[407] provides that "*the information regarding a client's or potential client's knowledge and experience in the investment field includes the following, to the extent appropriate:*

(a) the types of service, transaction and financial instrument with which the client is familiar;

(b) the nature, volume, and frequency of the client's transactions in financial instruments and the period over which they have been carried out; and

(c) the level of education, and profession or relevant former profession of the client or potential client."

Additional guidance on performing the appropriateness assessment is located at COBS 10A.2.7G to 10G.

Where the firm considers that the product or service is not appropriate for the client, or where the client has provided insufficient information for appropriateness to be properly assessed, the firm must warn the client accordingly. The firm can nonetheless go ahead with the transaction at

---

404 COBS 10A.6.

405 MiFID Org Regulation art. 56(1) (= COBS 10A.2.3UK).

406 MiFID Org Regulation art. 56(1) (= COBS 10A.2.3UK).

407 = COBS 10A.2.4R.

the client's request, but must give due consideration whether to do so having regard to the circumstances.[408]

11.4 Client Disclosures and Reporting

Principle 7 states: "*A firm must pay due regard to the information needs of its clients, and communicate information to them in a way which is clear, fair and not misleading.*"

FCA requirements in this area fall broadly into two groups: initial disclosures and ongoing reporting.

Various items of information which must be provided to clients are required to be done so in a "**durable medium**", which is defined as including paper or any compliant instrument (which may be provided by means of electronic communications) that is appropriate to the context and specifically chosen by the recipient.[409] Further, MiFID Org Regulation art. 3(2) and (3) prescribes conditions which must be satisfied if a firm wishes to provide certain specified types of information to clients by means of a website.[410]

Aside from the requirements considered below which originated in MiFID, many specific client disclosure and reporting obligations exist for other types of business, including AIFMs (see §13.2) and credit firms (see §13.3).

---

408 COBS 10A.3.

409 FCA Handbook Glossary; see also MiFID Org Regulation art. 3(1) and "Durable medium" (webpage, 2017).

410 A new MiFID Org Regulation art. 3(1B) is introduced by the Markets in Financial Instruments (Capital Markets) (Amendment) Regulations 2021, which effectively requires firms to provide information that must be provided to professional clients and eligible counterparties in a durable medium, in electronic format. Additionally, art. 3(2)(b) is amended so that only retail clients are required to specifically consent to the receipt of information by website (where that is permitted). These provisions came into force on 26 July 2021 but are not yet reflected in the FCA Handbook.

11.4.1 Client Initial Disclosures

A firm must provide appropriate information in good time[411] to a client with regard to:

- the firm and its services;
- the financial instruments and proposed investment strategies;
- execution venues; and
- all costs and related charges.[412]

The following additional specific requirements supplement these broad headings:

The firm and its services
• General information about the investment firm and its services for clients and potential clients, as listed in MiFID Org Regulation art. 47(1).[413] • Information about the firm's portfolio management service, as listed in MiFID Org Regulation art. 47(2) and (3).[414] • Information concerning safeguarding of financial instruments or funds belonging to clients, as listed in MiFID Org Regulation art. 49.[415]

411 COBS 1.2.5G.

412 COBS 2.2A.2R.

413 = COBS 6.1ZA.5UK.

414 = COBS 6.1ZA.8UK.

415 = COBS 6.1ZA.9UK.

• Restrictions and requirements when describing advice as "independent" or "non-independent", under MiFID Org Regulation arts. 52 and 53 and COBS 6.2B. • Written basic agreement with the client, setting out the essential rights and obligations of the firm and the client.[416] • Inducements.[417] • Information about the Financial Services Compensation Scheme.[418] • Any notices required under GDPR and telephone conversation recording rules – see §8.1.1 and §8.6.2.
The financial instruments and proposed investment strategies
• General description of the nature and risks of financial instruments, as listed in MiFID Org Regulation art. 48.[419]
Execution venues
• Appropriate information on the firm's order execution policy, including any possibility that client orders may be executed outside a trading venue.[420]

416 COBS 8A.1.4UK.

417 COBS 2.3A.10R.

418 COBS 6.1ZA.22R.

419 = COBS 14.3A.5UK.

420 COBS 11.2A.22R(1), 24R(1). For further details of the requirements governing a firm's order execution policy, see §11.5.

All costs and related charges
• Costs and associated charges information on an ex-ante basis, as listed in MiFID Org Regulation art. 50.[421] • For firms distributing units in collective investment undertakings or PRIIPs: additionally, (1) any other costs and associated charges related to the product which may have not been included in the UCITS Key Investor Information Document or PRIIPs Key Information Document, and (2) the costs and charges relating to the firm's provision of investment services in relation to that financial instrument.[422] • For firms which make personal recommendations to retail clients in relation to retail investment products: additionally, the adviser charging disclosures required under COBS 6.1A.24R to 26G.

421 = COBS 6.1ZA.14UK. Regarding aggregated third-party payments received: an itemised breakdown must be provided upon request, and it is considered best practice to inform a client of this right when providing the aggregated information (see "Questions and Answers On MiFID II and MiFIR investor protection and intermediaries topics" (ESMA35-43-349) (ESMA, 2021), Chapter 9 Q. 13). See also "Approach to Implementation for MiFID II Costs & Charges Disclosures" (Tax Incentivised Savings Association, 2017). A new MiFID Org Regulation art. 50(1A) is introduced by the Markets in Financial Instruments (Capital Markets) (Amendment) Regulations 2021, which effectively disapplies the costs and charges disclosure requirements for professional clients and eligible counterparties except in the context of portfolio management or investment advice. This provision came into force on 26 July 2021 but is not yet reflected in the FCA Handbook.

422 MiFID Org Regulation art. 51 (= COBS 14.3A.11UK).

Firms must also notify clients in good time about any material change to the information provided under MiFID Org Regulation arts. 47 to 50 (as indicated in the table above).[423]

11.4.2 Client Ongoing Reporting

A firm must provide a client with adequate reports on the service provided, including:

- periodic communications to the client, taking into account the type and the complexity of the financial instruments involved and the nature of the service provided to the client;[424]
- where applicable, the costs associated with the transactions and services undertaken on behalf of the client;[425]
- execution of orders other than when undertaking portfolio management;[426] and

[423] MiFID Org Regulation art. 46(4) (= COBS 6.1ZA.20UK and COBS 14.3A.10UK).

[424] COBS 16A.2.1R(2)(a). Nothing is added to this obligation by the requirement in COBS 11.2A.37R to inform the client of where the order was executed following the execution of a transaction: see "Markets in Financial Instruments Directive II Implementation – Policy Statement II" (PS17/14).

[425] COBS 16A.2.1R(2)(b). As with ex-ante costs and charges disclosures, technical requirements for ex-post disclosures are set out in MiFID Org Regulation art. 50 (= COBS 6.1ZA.14UK).

[426] COBS 16A.3.

- periodic reports from portfolio managers, and *ad hoc* notification of any depreciation by a multiple of 10% from the beginning of the reporting period.[427]

Where inducements are received in relation to the provision of independent advice, restricted advice or portfolio management services, the firm must inform the client about those inducements, such as through the periodic reporting statements.[428]

A firm that is an asset manager or asset owner carrying on TCFD in-scope business may be subject to an obligation to include public TCFD product reports on its main website (see §12.1.1). To the extent that this is the case, a firm must also include its public TCFD product report (or a cross-reference and hyperlink) in a relevant client report, and must provide on-demand TCFD product report or underlying asset data when requested by a client.[429]

11.5 Dealing and Managing

Where a firm's business involves dealing in or managing investments, various sets of rules apply which are designed to ensure that any trading on behalf of customers is done with due regard to customers' interests.

427 MiFID Org Regulation arts. 60 and 62; reproduced in COBS 16A.4.1UK and 3UK. MiFID Org Regulation art. 62(1) is amended by the Markets in Financial Instruments (Capital Markets) (Amendment) Regulations 2021 r. 3(10), which effectively removes the obligation for professional clients. This provision came into force on 26 July 2021 but is not yet reflected in COBS 16A.4.3UK.

428 COBS 2.3A.1R(3)(d).

429 ESG 2.3.1R and 5R.

11.5.1 Best Execution

When executing client orders, firms must comply with detailed requirements contained mainly in COBS 11.2A which are aimed at ensuring the best possible results for clients.[430]

For firms that place orders with other entities for execution in the course of portfolio management, and/or transmit client orders to other entities for execution in the course of providing the service of reception and transmission of orders, analogous requirements apply under MiFID Org Regulation art. 65 (= COBS 11.2A.34UK).

The best execution provisions require firms to (most notably):

Execution quality
• ... take all sufficient steps to obtain the best possible result for their clients[431] taking into account the execution factors,[432] the relative importance of which shall be determined by reference to the "relative importance" criteria.[433]

[430] Equivalent provisions for AIFMs and UCITS management companies are contained in COBS 11.2 and 11.2B respectively.

[431] COBS 11.2A.2R(1) (see also analogous requirement for portfolio managers (etc.) in MiFID Org Regulation art. 65(1), (2) = COBS 11.2A.34UK).

[432] The "**execution factors**" are "*price, costs, speed, likelihood of execution and settlement, size, nature or any other consideration relevant to the execution of the order*" (COBS 11.2A.2R(2); see also analogous requirement for portfolio managers (etc.) in MiFID Org Regulation art. 65(4) = COBS 11.2A.34UK).

[433] The "**relative importance criteria**" are "*(a) the characteristics of the client including the categorisation of the client as retail or professional; (b) the characteristics of the client order, including where the order involves a securities financing transaction (SFT); (c) the characteristics of financial instruments that are the subject of that order; (d) the characteristics of the execution venues to which that order can be directed*" (MiFID Org Regulation art. 64(1) = COBS 11.2A.8UK; also incorporated by reference, for portfolio managers (etc.), in MiFID Org Regulation art. 65(4) = COBS 11.2A.34UK).

Order execution arrangements and order execution policy
• ... establish and implement effective arrangements for complying with the obligation to take all sufficient steps to obtain the best possible results for its clients, including establishing and implementing an order execution policy for this purpose.[434]
Information to clients
• ... provide appropriate information to its clients on its order execution policy.[435] • ... obtain prior consent of its clients to the order execution policy.[436] • ... inform clients about any possibility that client orders may be executed outside a trading venue, and obtain express prior consent before proceeding to so execute.[437] • ... notify clients of any material changes to its order execution arrangements or execution policy.[438]

434 COBS 11.2A.20R, with guidance in COBS 11.2A.21R, 26G, 28G, 29G (see also analogous requirements for portfolio managers (etc.) in MiFID Org Regulation art. 65(5) and (6) = COBS 11.2A.34UK). Further detailed specifications are set out in MiFID Org Regulation art. 66 = COBS 11.2A.25UK (also incorporated by reference, for portfolio managers (etc.), in MiFID Org Regulation art. 65(6) = COBS 11.2A.34UK).

435 COBS 11.2A.22R (see also analogous requirement in MiFID Org Regulation art. 65(6) = COBS 11.2A.34UK). Further detailed specifications are set out in MiFID Org Regulation art. 66 = COBS 11.2A.25UK (also incorporated by reference, for portfolio managers (etc.), in MiFID Org Regulation art. 65(6) = COBS 11.2A.34UK).

436 COBS 11.2A.23R.

437 COBS 11.2A.24R.

438 COBS 11.2A.31R(2).

Information on execution quality
• ... be able to demonstrate to its clients, at their request, that it has executed their orders in accordance with its execution policy.[439] • ... be able to demonstrate to the FCA, at its request, its compliance with its obligation to execute orders on terms most favourable to the client.[440]
Monitoring and review
• ... monitor on a regular basis the effectiveness of the order execution policy and, in particular, monitor the execution quality of the entities identified in that policy and, where appropriate, correct any deficiencies, taking into account relevant data or other internal analyses conducted by investment firms.[441] • ... review order execution policy and arrangements at least annually, or whenever a material change occurs that affects the firm's ability to continue to obtain the best possible result for its clients.[442]

439 COBS 11.2A.32R(1).

440 COBS 11.2A.32R(2).

441 COBS 11.2A.31R(1) (see also analogous requirement for portfolio managers (etc.) in MiFID Org Regulation art. 65(7) = COBS 11.2A.34UK). Firms should conduct both ex-ante and ex-post monitoring, as described in "Questions and Answers On MiFID II and MiFIR investor protection and intermediaries topics" (ESMA35-43-349) (ESMA, 2021), Chapter 1 Q. 1.

442 MiFID Org Regulation art. 66(1) = COBS 11.2A.25UK (see also analogous requirement for portfolio managers (etc.) in MiFID Org Regulation art. 65(6) = COBS 11.2A.34UK).

The FCA has conducted much industry research on this topic in recent years and published relevant material including "Investment managers still failing to ensure effective oversight of best execution" (webpage, 2021) and "Best execution and payment for order flow" (TR14/13).

11.5.2 Client Order Handling: General Principles

Under COBS 11.3.1R, a firm which is authorised to execute orders on behalf of clients must implement procedures and arrangements which provide for the prompt, fair and expeditious execution of client orders, relative to other orders or the trading interests of the firm, which must allow for the execution of otherwise comparable orders in accordance with the time of their reception by the firm.

More specifically, when carrying out client orders, firms must:

- ensure that orders executed on behalf of clients are promptly and accurately recorded and allocated;

- carry out otherwise comparable client orders sequentially and promptly unless the characteristics of the order or prevailing market conditions make this impracticable, or the interests of the client require otherwise; and

- where an order is for a retail client, inform the retail client about any relevant material difficulty promptly upon becoming aware of the difficulty.[443]

Firms responsible for overseeing or arranging the settlement of an executed order must take all reasonable steps to ensure that any client financial instruments or client funds received in settlement of that executed order are promptly and correctly delivered to the account of the appropriate client.[444]

---

[443] MiFID Org Regulation art. 67(1) = COBS 11.3.2AUK.

[444] MiFID Org Regulation art. 67(2) = COBS 11.3.4AUK.

Finally, firms must not misuse information relating to pending client orders, and must take all reasonable steps to prevent the misuse of such information by any of its relevant persons.[445]

11.5.3 Client Order Handling: Aggregation and Allocation

A firm must not carry out a client order in aggregation with another client order unless:

- it is unlikely that the aggregation of orders and transactions will work overall to the disadvantage of any client whose order is to be aggregated;
- it is disclosed to each client whose order is to be aggregated that the effect of aggregation may work to its disadvantage in relation to a particular order; and
- an order allocation policy is established and effectively implemented, providing for the fair allocation of aggregated orders and transactions, including how the volume and price of orders determine allocations and the treatment of partial executions.[446]

Where a firm aggregates an order with one or more other client orders and the aggregated order is partially executed, it must allocate the related trades in accordance with its order allocation policy.[447]

When aggregating transactions for own account with one or more client orders, the firm must not allocate the related trades in a way that is detrimental to a client, and must allocate partial executions to the client

---

445 MiFID Org Regulation art. 67(3) = COBS 11.3.5AUK.

446 MiFID Org Regulation art. 68(1) = COBS 11.3.7AUK.

447 MiFID Org Regulation art. 68(2) = COBS 11.3.8AUK.

in priority to the firm. Procedures to ensure compliance with these requirements must be included in the firm's order allocation policy.[448]

11.5.4 Client Limit Orders

Where a client limit order in respect of shares admitted to trading on a regulated market or traded on a trading venue is not immediately executed under prevailing market conditions, a firm must in principle take measures to facilitate the earliest possible execution of that order by making public immediately that client limit order in a manner which is easily accessible to other market participants.[449]

However, this obligation to make client limit orders public does not apply if:

- a client expressly instructs otherwise;[450] or
- the relevant transaction is large in scale compared with normal market size (as determined under MiFIR art. 4).[451]

11.6 Complaints

In broad terms, a "**complaint**" is defined as any oral or written expression of dissatisfaction, whether justified or not, from a person about the provision of, or failure to provide, a financial service.

---

448 MiFID Org Regulation art. 69 = COBS 11.3.9AUK to 11AUK.

449 COBS 11.4.1R. Methods for "**making public**" are described in MiFID Org Regulation art. 70(1) = COBS 11.4.3AUK.

450 COBS 11.4.1R.

451 COBS 11.4.5R.

Where the complaint relates to an investment firm's provision (or failure to provide) investments services to a MiFID client, this will be treated as a "**MiFID complaint**".[452]

A firm's obligations in relation to dealing with complaints are set out mainly in DISP. Complaints that remain unresolved may in certain circumstances come within the jurisdiction of the Financial Ombudsman Service.[453]

11.6.1 MiFID Complaints

Regarding MiFID complaints, a firm must:

- Publish the details of the process to be followed when handling a MiFID complaint.[454]

- Establish, implement and maintain effective and transparent complaints management policies and procedures for the prompt handling of clients' or potential clients' MiFID complaints.[455]

- Handle MiFID complaints in accordance with the complaints resolution requirements of DISP 1.1A.20R to 36R.

- Keep a record of the complaints received and the measures taken for their resolution.[456]

---

452 See also DISP 1.1A.3G.

453 DISP 2.

454 MiFID Org Regulation art. 26(2) (= DISP 1.1A.10UK).

455 MiFID Org Regulation art. 26(1) para. 1 (= DISP 1.1A.12UK).

456 MiFID Org Regulation art. 26(1) para. 1 (= DISP 1.1A.37UK).

- Provide the FCA with biannual complaints reports[457] including (if reporting 500 or more complaints) a complaints data summary.[458]

11.6.2 Non-MiFID Complaints

As a general matter, the FCA's rules for dealing with complaints other than MiFID complaints apply only to the extent that a firm receives complaints from "eligible complainants".[459]

To be an "**eligible complainant**", a person must:

- fall within a prescribed category of person – most notably: consumer; micro-enterprise; charity; or trustee;[460] and

- have a relevant relationship with the firm (*e.g.*, as its customer). A fund investor can also be an eligible complainant against a firm, but only if the firm is the operator of the fund (*e.g.*, as AIFM), and not only a discretionary investment manager.[461]

In relation to complaints from eligible complainants, firms must comply with rules that are analogous to those for MiFID complaints and which are set out in DISP 1.2 to 10.

---

457 DISP 1.10 (as modified by DISP 1.1A.39R in order to refer to retail clients, professional clients, and (where relevant) eligible counterparties rather than eligible complainants).

458 DISP 1.10A (as clarified by DISP 1.1A.41G to the effect that a firm's complaints data summary should include relevant data about any MiFID complaints received by the firm).

459 DISP 1.1.3R.

460 DISP 2.7.3R.

461 DISP 2.7.6R.

12 WEBSITE, PUBLICITY AND MARKETING

Various regulatory regimes apply to firms wishing to market products or distributing promotional materials in the UK.

Firms should be mindful too of the relevant wider law in this area (such as in relation to misrepresentation and misstatement), as well as the codes and rulings of the principal self-regulatory organisation for the advertising industry in the UK, the Advertising Standards Authority.[462] Marketing and publicity that reach overseas recipients may also fall within local legal and regulatory regimes. All these topics are beyond the scope of this book.

One important aspect of a control framework for marketing and publicity is the inclusion of appropriate disclosures and disclaimers on promotional materials. Such wording should be prepared with a view to mitigating legal risk (*e.g.*, the risk of mis-selling or negligence claims) as well as regulatory risk (*e.g.*, the risk of breaching the "fair, clear and not misleading" rule or the restriction on promoting fund products). It is worth highlighting that, where information is in the nature of a risk disclosure, it must use "*a font size... that is at least equal to the predominant font size used throughout the information provided*":[463] in other words, the "small print" in promotional materials should not be small.

12.1 Public Disclosures

Where a firm has a website and sends corporate emails, certain technical disclosures must (or should) be made in order to comply with applicable

[462] See "Memorandum of Understanding between the Financial Conduct Authority and the Advertising Standards Authority" (FCA and Advertising Standards Authority, 2019).

[463] MiFID Org Regulation art. 44(1)(c).

requirements – some financial regulatory, and others relevant to financial and non-financial businesses alike.

There are also various rules that require a firm to publish items of information about itself and its services. This is often most conveniently achieved by uploading such information to the firm's website; indeed, where the firm has a website, it may be mandatory to use it for such publications.

Notable requirements that may be relevant to firms are summarised below. Separately, firms should also bear in mind that websites can constitute or contain promotional material, and to that extent firms should consider including on their websites disclaimers and disclosures that are similar to those they use generally with other forms of promotional material.

12.1.1 Regulatory Information for Websites

Item	Legislative ref.
Prescribed information about the firm and its products or services.[464]	COBS 5.2.2R to 4R

464 Under COBS 5.2.1R, this obligation is applicable to the extent that the firm carries on an electronic commerce activity with or for a person in the UK.

"**Electronic commerce activity**" means "*an activity which: (a) consists of the provision of an information society service from an establishment in the UK; and (b) is a regulated activity*".

The meaning of "**information society service**" is, in turn, summarised as "*any service normally provided for remuneration, at a distance, by means of electronic equipment for the processing (including the digital compression) and storage of data at the individual request of a service recipient*". Government guidance confirms that this definition can include "*offering online information or commercial communications (e.g., adverts) or providing tools allowing for search, access and retrieval of data*" ("A Guide for Business to the Electronic Commerce (EC Directive) Regulations 2002 (SI 2002/2013)" (Department of Trade and Industry, 2002)).

Commitment (or otherwise) to the Financial Reporting Council's Stewardship Code.	COBS 2.2.3R, 2.2A.5R
Engagement policy. (Applies only to certain types of firm including UK firms providing portfolio management services, UK UCITS management companies and full-scope UK AIFMs.)	COBS 2.2B.8R
Complaints procedure.	DISP 1.1A.10UK
Financial Services Compensation Scheme information (if not made available in a durable medium).	COBS 6.1ZA.22R
Risk management objectives and policies. (Applies only to non-SNI MIFIDPRU investment firms, and SNI MIFIDPRU investment firms that have additional tier 1 instruments in issue.)	MIFIDPRU 8.2[465]
Governance. (Applies only to non-SNI MIFIDPRU investment firms.)	MIFIDPRU 8.3
Own funds. (Applies only to non-SNI MIFIDPRU investment firms, and SNI MIFIDPRU investment firms that have additional tier 1 instruments in issue.)	MIFIDPRU 8.4

465 General rules governing the format, timing and method of MIFIDPRU disclosures are set out in MIFIDPRU 8.1.

Own funds requirements. (Applies only to non-SNI MIFIDPRU investment firms, and SNI MIFIDPRU investment firms that have additional tier 1 instruments in issue.)	MIFIDPRU 8.5
Remuneration policy.	MIFIDPRU 8.6
Investment policy. (Applies only to non-SNI MIFIDPRU investment firms that do not fall within MIFIDPRU 7.1.4R(1).)	MIFIDPRU 8.7
TCFD entity report. (Applies to asset managers and asset owners, in relation to TCFD in-scope business (such as portfolio management and managing an AIF), subject to exemption in ESG 1.2.2R and transitional provisions in ESG TP 1.)	ESG 2.1, 2.2
Public TCFD product report. (Applies to asset managers and asset owners, in relation to TCFD in-scope business (such as portfolio management and managing an AIF), subject to exemption in ESG 1.2.2R and transitional provisions in ESG TP 1.)	ESG 2.1, 2.3

12.1.2 General Corporate Information for Websites

Item	Legislative ref.
Prescribed particulars of the company.	Company, Limited Liability Partnership and Business (Names and Trading Disclosures) Regulations 2015 r. 25
Section 172(1) statement.	Companies Act 2006 ss.172(1), 414CZA, 426B
Statement of private company governance arrangements (only if either: (a) more than 2,000 employees; or (b) turnover >£200 million and balance sheet >£2 billion).	Large and Medium-sized Companies and Groups (Accounts and Reports) Regulations 2008 Sch.7 Part 8
Privacy notice.	GDPR arts. 13, 14
Cookies notice.	Privacy and Electronic Communications (EC Directive) Regulations 2002 r. 6
Slavery and human trafficking statement (if turnover >£36m).	Modern Slavery Act 2015 s. 54(7)
Gender pay gap information (if over 250 employees).	Equality Act 2010 (Gender Pay Gap Information) Regulations 2017 r. 15
Tax strategy disclosure (if turnover >£200m or balance sheet >£2bn).	Finance Act 2016 s. 161 and Schedule 19

Web accessibility statement (voluntary).	Equality Act 2010 s. 20(6)
Covid-19 health and safety risk assessment (expected if >50 employees).	"Working safely during coronavirus (COVID-19)" (UK Government webpage, 2020)

12.1.3 Regulatory and General Corporate Information for Emails

Item	**Legislative ref.**
Prescribed particulars of the company.	Company, Limited Liability Partnership and Business (Names and Trading Disclosures) Regulations 2015 r. 25
Privacy notice.	GDPR arts. 13, 14
For unsolicited commercial communication: clear and unambiguous identification as an unsolicited commercial communication.	COBS 5.2.5R

12.2 Communicating with Clients and Potential Clients

12.2.1 Communications in Relation to Investment Business

Where a firm's communications to its clients or potential clients relate to its investment business – likely, in practice, to cover most of its client communications – COBS 4.2.1R(1) requires the firm to "*ensure that a communication or a financial promotion is fair, clear and not misleading*" (the "'**fair, clear and not misleading' rule**"). A firm that takes reasonable steps to ensure it complies with the "fair, clear and not misleading" rule will have a defence to a statutory action for damages.[466]

FCA guidance provides that the "fair, clear and not misleading" rule "*applies in a way that is appropriate and proportionate taking into account the means of communication, the information the communication is intended to convey and the nature of the client and of its business, if any*".[467]

A more specific requirement exists for firms to "*ensure that any reference in advertising to an investor compensation scheme*[468] *is limited to a factual reference to the scheme*".[469]

12.2.2 Provision of Information

Where a firm addresses information to, or disseminates information in such a way that it is likely to be received by, a current or potential retail or professional client, it must ensure that all such information complies with MiFID Org Regulation art. 44,[470] the provisions of which fall within the following headings:

- General requirements;
- Comparative information;
- Referring to tax;
- Consistent financial promotions;

---

466 COBS 4.2.6R.

467 COBS 4.2.2G(1).

468 *E.g.*, the Financial Services Compensation Scheme.

469 COBS 4.4.1R.

470 = COBS 4.5A.3UK to 16UK.

- Past performance;
- Simulated past performance;
- Future performance; and
- Information that uses the name of any competent authority.

These provisions build upon the "fair, clear and not misleading" rule described in §12.2.1. Exempted from these requirements are any communications that constitute a third-party prospectus or image advertising.[471]

12.2.3 Financial Promotions

A further layer of rules applies where a firm communicates a "**financial promotion**" – defined as an "*invitation or inducement to engage in investment activity that is communicated in the course of business*".[472]

Under FSMA s. 21, the communication of a financial promotion in the course of business is permissible only if:

- done by an authorised person; or

---

471 COBS 4.5A.1R(2). "**Third party prospectus**" is defined as (essentially) "*a communication made by a firm if the communication is a prospectus that… has been approved by the FCA in accordance with Part 6 of the Act and the firm is not responsible under the Prospectus Rules for the information given in the prospectus*".

"**Image advertising**" is defined as "*a communication that consists only of one or more of the following: (a) the name of the firm; (b) a logo or other image associated with the firm; (c) a contact point; and (d) a reference to the types of regulated activities provided by the firm, or to its fees or commissions*".

472 For guidance on meaning and scope, see PERG 8 (especially PERG 8.1 to 22, 36).

- duly approved by an authorised person;[473] or
- done in exempt circumstances as specified by statutory instrument.

Contravention of this restriction is a criminal offence under FSMA s. 25, and certain agreements entered into as a result of such unlawful communication may be rendered unenforceable under s. 30.

As authorised persons, regulated firms are able to communicate financial promotions regardless of which activities are included in their scope of permission. However, firms must comply with applicable FCA rules – most notably, the "**financial promotion rules**" in COBS 4 – when communicating financial promotions.

The main components of the financial promotion rules are the requirements described in §12.2.1 and §12.2.2. Additionally, firms should ensure that financial promotions take account of the guidance at COBS 4.2.4G (which supplements the "fair, clear and not misleading" rule insofar as it relates to financial promotions), and that financial promotions addressed to a client are clearly identifiable as such.[474] The FCA has also issued specific guidance on making financial promotions in social media.[475]

Enhanced requirements apply to two subsets of financial promotions: direct offer financial promotions;[476] and cold calls and other promotions that are not in writing.[477]

---

473 For guidance, see "Approving financial promotions" (webpage, 2021).

474 COBS 4.3.1R.

475 "Social media and customer communications: The FCA's supervisory approach to financial promotions in social media" (FG15/4).

476 See MiFID Org Regulation art. 46(6) (= COBS 4.7.-1AUK).

477 See COBS 4.8.

12.3 Product Regimes

A general product governance regime applies to investment firms that manufacture or distribute financial instruments. Supplemental regimes may additionally apply in relation to certain specific types of products and services. The principal features of the general regime and some notable supplemental regimes are considered below.

12.3.1 Product Governance

A firm must, when manufacturing financial instruments or deciding on the range of financial instruments and investment services it intends to distribute to clients, comply, in a way that is appropriate and proportionate, with applicable product governance requirements.[478]

A firm that is a product manufacturer[479] must (in summary):

- ensure that the financial instruments it manufactures are designed to meet the needs of an identified target market of end-clients within the relevant category of clients;
- ensure that the strategy for distribution of the financial instruments is compatible with the identified target market; and
- take reasonable steps to ensure that the financial instrument is distributed to the identified target market.[480]

A firm that is a product distributor[481] must (in summary):

478 PROD 3.1.2R(1).

479 "**Manufacturer**" is defined as "*a firm which creates, develops, issues, and/or designs investments, including when advising corporate issuers on the launch of new investments*".

480 PROD 3.2.1R.

481 "**Distributor**" is defined as "*a firm which offers, recommends or sells investments or provides investment services to clients*".

- understand the financial instruments it distributes to clients;
- assess the compatibility of the financial instruments with the needs of the clients to whom it distributes investment services, taking into account the manufacturer's identified target market of end clients; and
- ensure that financial instruments are distributed only when this is in the best interests of the client.[482]

A template providing a functional description of the minimum set of data (defining a product's target market and disclosing its costs and charges) has been published by the European Fund and Asset Management Association ("**EFAMA**"), which firms are free to use and may find helpful when addressing their product governance requirements.[483]

12.3.2 Collective Investment Schemes

Promoting and marketing fund products have long been deemed by policymakers to present enhanced consumer protection risks. As a result, authorised firms – which are otherwise free in principle to communicate financial promotions – are subject to specific statutory restrictions when it comes to promoting or marketing fund products.

Under FSMA s. 238, an authorised person must not communicate an invitation or inducement to participate in a collective investment scheme[484] unless the collective investment scheme is (most notably):

---

[482] PROD 3.3.1R.

[483] "European MiFID Template (EMT)" (EFAMA, 2017).

[484] "**Collective investment scheme**" is defined as "*any arrangements with respect to property of any description, including money, the purpose or effect of which is to enable persons taking part in the arrangements (whether by becoming owners of the property or any part of it or otherwise) to participate in or receive profits or income*

- a "**regulated collective investment scheme**", defined as comprising "**authorised funds**" (*i.e.*, ICVC, AUT and ACS) and recognised schemes;[485] or

- promoted in exempt circumstances as specified by FCA rules or statutory instrument.

Regulated collective investment schemes may, in principle, be promoted to the general public (including retail clients),[486] subject to compliance with the financial promotion rules (see §12.2.3). However, such promotions are subject to the product regulation regime set out in COLL (and supplemented by additional guidance in COLLG), which includes detailed operational, formal and informational requirements. Where a regulated collective investment scheme is a UCITS within the meaning of FSMA ss. 236A and 237 ("**UK UCITS**" or "**UCITS**"), additional marketing rules in COBS 4.13 apply.[487]

All other collective investment schemes are "**unregulated collective investment schemes**". These may be promoted only in accordance with the exemptions in (1) the Financial Services and Markets Act 2000 (Promotion of Collective Investment Schemes) (Exemptions) Order 2001, or (2) COBS 4.12, which sets out restrictions and exemptions applicable to the promotion of non-mainstream pooled investments. "**Non-mainstream pooled investments**" are defined as including

---

arising from the acquisition, holding, management or disposal of the property or sums paid out of such profits or income" (FSMA s. 235(1)), but subject to various significant exclusions.

485 FCA Handbook Glossary; see also FSMA s. 238(4). "**Recognised schemes**" are defined (essentially) as comprising: individually recognised overseas schemes under FSMA s. 272; and EEA UCITS schemes recognised under the Collective Investment Schemes (Amendment etc.) (EU Exit) Regulations 2019 Part 6.

486 Except for QIS, which (as non-mainstream pooled investments) may be promoted only in accordance with the restrictions and exemptions set out in COBS 4.12.

487 Further guidance is available at "Authorised and recognised funds" (webpage, 2021).

unregulated collective investment schemes as well as "qualified investor schemes" within COLL 8 ("**QIS**") and certain other types of products.

To the extent that a firm wishes to promote a non-mainstream pooled investment to an elective professional client in accordance with a relevant exemption, it is worth noting that in principle promotional activity falls outside the scope of MiFID business and accordingly the "quantitative test" in COBS 3.5.3R(2) does not apply.

Many non-mainstream pooled investments constitute AIFs, which are subject to management and marketing obligations that are considered in §13.2.

12.3.3 Packaged Retail and Insurance-Based Investment Products

Under the PRIIPs Regulation, a "**packaged retail and insurance-based investment product**" ("**PRIIP**") is defined as "*a product that is one or both of the following: (a) a PRIP; (b) an insurance-based investment product*". In turn:

- "**PRIP**" (or "**packaged retail investment product**") is defined as "*an investment, including instruments issued by special purpose vehicles as defined in [Solvency II Directive] or securitisation special purpose entities as defined in [AIFMD], where, regardless of the legal form of the investment, the amount repayable to the retail investor is subject to fluctuations because of exposure to reference values or to the performance of one or more assets which are not directly purchased by the retail investor*"; and
- "**insurance-based investment product**" is defined as "*an insurance product which offers a maturity or surrender value and where that maturity or surrender value is wholly or partially exposed, directly or indirectly, to market fluctuations*".[488]

---

[488] PRIIPs Regulation art. 4.

The FCA considers that the definition of a PRIIP is wide enough to cover regulated and unregulated collective investment schemes (including, in each case, both those which are and those which are not also AIFs), as well as many other retail products.[489]

A firm is within scope of the PRIIPs Regulation to the extent that it manufactures, advises on or sells a PRIIP to or for retail investors. In such cases, the firm must comply with the applicable product regulation regime set out in the PRIIPs Regulation and PRIIPs KID RTS, including (most notably) the obligation to produce a key information document that conforms to the prescribed technical specifications.[490]

12.3.4 Complex Investment Products and Speculative Illiquid Securities

Firms should be aware of the restrictions in COBS 22 on distributing certain complex investment products[491] and, in COBS 4.14, on promoting speculative illiquid securities[492] to retail investors.

Where restrictions apply, typically they mean that mass-marketing is precluded because firms are prohibited from communicating or approving a relevant financial promotion where that financial promotion is addressed to, or disseminated in such a way that it is likely to be received by, a retail client. Additionally, there may be prescriptive form

---

489 "PRIIPs disclosure: Key Information Documents" (webpage, 2018).

490 PRIIPs Regulation arts. 5, 13.

491 Comprising: mutual society shares; contingent convertible instruments and CoCo funds; derivative contracts of a binary or other fixed outcomes nature; contracts for differences and similar speculative investments; and cryptoasset derivatives and cryptoasset exchange traded notes.

492 "**Speculative illiquid securities**" are defined as (in summary) debentures or preference shares which (1) have a denomination or minimum investment of less than £100,000, and (2) are issued for a financing purpose as specified in COBS 4.14.20R.

or content requirements that permitted financial promotions must comply with.

13 SECTOR-SPECIFIC REGIMES

Outlined below are supplemental operational and conduct regimes for firms that trade securities or are authorised as AIFMs or credit firms.

Other types of firm (which are beyond the scope of this book) may find regimes relevant to them located in COBS 18 or the "Specialist sourcebooks" block of the FCA Handbook.

13.1 Securities Trading

Numerous regulatory and securities markets regimes around the world impose limits and obligations upon firms that trade financial instruments. Considered below is a sample of key regulatory regimes applicable to investment firms trading in the UK.

13.1.1 Pre-Trade Regimes

Regime	Summary of key obligations
Share trading obligation (MiFIR art. 23)	For shares admitted to trading on a regulated market or traded on a trading venue, firms may only trade such shares on a regulated market, MTF, SI, or third-country venue assessed as equivalent to a UK regulated market.
Derivatives trading obligation (MiFIR art. 28)	Firms may only trade in-scope derivatives on a regulated market, MTF, OTF or third-country venue assessed as equivalent to a UK regulated market. Derivatives in scope are (in summary) those that: (1) have been declared subject to the clearing obligation under EMIR; (2) are admitted to trading or traded on at least one UK trading venue (a regulated market, MTF, OTF or a third country equivalent trading venue); and (3) are sufficiently liquid.

	Counterparties within scope are, in principle, the same as those in scope for mandatory central clearing under EMIR art. 4.
Restrictions on uncovered short selling and sovereign CDS (Short Selling Regulation arts. 12 to 14)	For: • issued shares of companies admitted to trading on a regulated market or MTF and their derivatives; and • UK sovereign debt, a firm must not engage in short selling unless (in summary) the securities have been borrowed, an agreement has been entered into for the securities to be borrowed, or "locate arrangements" are in place. (The FCA may temporarily suspend or extend these restrictions in certain circumstances.) Uncovered UK sovereign CDS (credit default swaps) are prohibited (although the FCA may temporarily suspend the prohibition in certain circumstances).
Short selling / short position bans in exceptional circumstances (Short Selling Regulation arts. 20, 21)	Prohibition/conditions on short sales or similar transactions, where there are "*adverse events or developments which constitute a serious threat to financial stability or to market confidence in the United Kingdom*".
Short selling bans in case of significant fall in price (Short Selling Regulation art. 23)	Prohibition on short selling for one trading day in the case of a significant fall in price of a financial instrument. A "**significant fall in price**" means 10% or more in the case of a liquid share, and, for illiquid shares and other classes of financial instruments, an amount to be specified by HM Treasury.

OTC derivatives trading: risk-mitigation techniques (EMIR art. 11(1) to (4); EMIR Delegated Regulation)	When trading OTC derivatives: ensure, exercising due diligence, that appropriate procedures and arrangements are in place to measure, monitor and mitigate operational risk and counterparty credit risk. These include the following prescribed risk-mitigation techniques: timely confirms; portfolio reconciliation; portfolio compression; dispute resolution; regulatory reporting of unconfirmed transactions; daily mark-to-market; regulatory reporting of unresolved disputes; collateral exchange procedures; minimum capital requirements.[493]
Commodity derivatives position limits (MAR 10.2)	Commodity derivatives holders must comply at all times with position limits published by the FCA. These are limits on the size of net positions in commodity derivatives traded on UK trading venues and economically equivalent OTC contracts that a person may hold at any time, aggregated together with any holdings of other members of the person's group. "**Commodity derivatives**" are defined widely to include, in summary, physically and cash-settled contracts that relate to a commodity, currencies, interest rates, climatic variables, freight rates or inflation rates (among others).
Takeover bids (City Code on Takeovers and Mergers, Rule 8)	For shares in UK companies admitted to trading on a UK regulated market or MTF: rules may in certain circumstances prohibit an acquisition of interests in shares or sometimes delay or limit the number of shares (or interests in shares) which may be acquired or stipulate consequences for the terms and value of an offer depending on the level of purchases.

493 Technical guidance is set out in "Questions and Answers – Implementation of the Regulation (EU) No 648/2012 on OTC derivatives, central counterparties and trade repositories (EMIR)" (ESMA70-1861941480-52) (ESMA, 2021).

13.1.2 Post-Trade Regimes

Regime	Summary of key obligations
Transaction reporting to FCA (MiFIR art. 26)[494]	For any financial instrument admitted to trading on a UK trading venue (whether or not the transaction was carried out on such a venue) or related OTC derivative: a firm must report details of transactions to FCA directly or via an approved reporting mechanism ("**ARM**") no later than the close of the following working day. Where a firm engages an ARM, if there are reporting failures which "*are attributable to the ARM [then] the ARM... shall be responsible for those failures.*" Instead of reporting directly or via an ARM, a firm could instead rely on its brokers to make such reports – but would then need to comply with onerous conditions relating to order transmission.
Post-trade transparency (MiFIR arts. 20, 21; RTS 1, 2)	For shares and equity-like and non-equity instruments, admitted to trading on a UK venue, when a trade is concluded outside a UK venue: • If the firm is buyer, must publish trade unless seller is SI or MiFID firm. • If the firm is seller, must publish trade unless buyer is SI.

494 Technical guidance is set out in "Final Report – Guidelines on Transaction reporting, order record keeping and clock synchronisation under MiFID II" (ESMA/2016/1452) (ESMA, 2016) and "Questions and Answers on MiFIR data reporting" (ESMA70-1861941480-56) (ESMA, 2021).

	Publication must be within 1 minute (in the case of shares and equity-like instruments) or 5 minutes (in the case of non-equity instruments) of execution. The FCA may grant waivers from the publication requirement for specific instruments. Any publication must be done at firm level, via an approved publication arrangement ("**APA**").
Commodity derivatives position reporting (MAR 10.4)	A firm must comply with position reporting obligations where it trades economically equivalent OTC contracts on commodity derivatives.
Short selling disclosures: shares (Short Selling Regulation arts. 5, 6)	For issued shares of companies admitted to trading on a UK regulated market or MTF and their derivatives: a firm must disclose to the FCA net short positions, subject to an initial threshold of (usually) 0.1%. Additional, public, disclosure obligations apply from an initial threshold of (usually) 0.5%.
Short selling disclosures: UK sovereign debt and uncovered CDS (Short Selling Regulation arts. 7 to 9)	For UK sovereign debt: a firm must disclose to the FCA net short positions, subject to initial thresholds of 0.5%.[495] The same obligation (with the same thresholds) applies to uncovered UK sovereign CDS (to the extent that the usual prohibition on entering into an uncovered UK sovereign CDS has been temporarily suspended).
Notification of major shareholdings (DTR 5)	For shares in UK companies admitted to trading on a regulated or prescribed market: a firm must notify the issuer of the percentage of voting rights it holds as shareholder (or holds or is deemed to hold through its direct or indirect holding of financial instruments) if,

495 This threshold is reviewed quarterly and any updates are published on "Notification and disclosure of net short positions" (webpage, 2021).

	as a result of an acquisition or disposal of shares or financial instruments, the percentage of those voting rights reaches, exceeds or falls below the applicable thresholds in DTR 5.1.2R or 5R.[496] Analogous rules may be applicable in other jurisdictions for non-UK shares.
OTC derivatives trading: mandatory clearing (EMIR art. 4(1); EMIR Delegated Regulation)	Clear eligible OTC derivatives contracts, to the extent that a counterparty is in scope.
OTC and listed derivatives trading: reporting (EMIR art. 9(1), (3); EMIR Implementing Regulation; EMIR Delegated Regulation)	Ensure that details of derivative contracts concluded and of any modification or termination are reported to a trade repository or (if not available) the FCA.
Securities financing transactions: conditions for re-use of collateral (SFTR art. 15)	A receiving counterparty must comply with applicable conditions before, and in the course of, exercising a right to reuse financial instruments received as collateral.

[496] Both the person subject to the notification obligations (termed "**Position Holder**") and the individuals submitting the relevant notification forms on their behalf (termed "**Reporting Persons**" or "**Position Holder Individuals**") must register with the FCA's Electronic Submission System.

Securities financing transactions: reporting (SFTR art. 4)	Ensure that details of securities financing transactions concluded and of any modification or termination are reported to a registered or recognised trade repository.
Portfolio compression (MiFIR Delegated Regulation arts. 17, 18)	Investment firms and market operators providing portfolio compression must comply with applicable conditions before initiating a compression process.
Takeover bids (City Code on Takeovers and Mergers, Rule 8)	For shares in UK companies admitted to trading on a UK regulated market or MTF: in the context of a takeover bid, once an offer period has commenced, disclosure of certain positions and dealings in relevant securities in a securities exchange bidder (that is, a bidder other than a cash bidder) and the target is required.
Requests from public companies (Companies Act 2006 s. 793)	For shares in UK public companies: where a firm receives a "s. 793 notice" from a UK public company investigating who has an interest in its issued share capital, the firm must respond or risk committing a criminal offence.

Firms seeking reference data about financial instruments and counterparties in connection with satisfying their securities trading obligations should familiarise themselves with regulatory databases such as the FCA's FIRDS (Financial Instruments Reference Data System) and FITRS (Financial Instruments Transparency Reference System), and the "Other Registers section" of the FS Register (which includes the Investment Firms Register, DRSP/MTF/OTF/SI Register, and Derivatives Trading Obligation Register).

13.2 Alternative Investment Fund Managers

13.2.1 Full-Scope UK AIFMs

The supplemental requirements for full-scope UK AIFMs are contained principally in FUND 3 and the AIFM Regulations (which were originally introduced to transpose AIFMD). More detailed technical specifications are set out in the AIFMD Level 2 Regulation, the relevant provisions of which are cross-referenced in FUND 3.

Both the management and the marketing of AIFs are governed by these requirements. For these purposes, an AIFM "**markets**" an AIF when it "*makes a direct or indirect offering or placement of units or shares of an AIF managed by it to or with an investor domiciled or with a registered office in the United Kingdom or Gibraltar, or when another person makes such an offering or placement at the initiative of, or on behalf of, the AIFM*".[497] Importantly, the restrictions on marketing "*do not apply to an offering or placement of units or shares of an AIF to an investor made at the initiative of that investor*" (a fact-pattern commonly referred to as "reverse solicitation").[498]

FUND 3 covers the following topics:

FUND 3 ref.	Relevant for full-scope UK AIFMs that...	Topic
2 (Investor information)	... manage UK AIFs or market AIFs in the UK	Prescribed information to be disclosed to AIF investors (1) before they invest, and (2) periodically.[499]

497 AIFM Regulations r. 45.

498 AIFM Regulations r. 47.

499 For AIFMs that make use of securities financing transactions and total return swaps, the disclosure should include information prescribed under SFTR art. 14.

3 (Annual report of an AIF)	… manage UK AIFs or market AIFs in the UK	Prescribed information to be included in annual reports which must be made available to investors and the FCA no later than six months after each financial year.[500]
4 (Reporting obligations to the FCA)	… manage UK AIFs or market AIFs in the UK	Periodic AIFM and AIF transparency reports: see §5.2.2.
5 (Investment in securitisation positions)	… manage UK AIFs	Obligation to take corrective action where the AIFM is exposed to a securitisation that does not meet the requirements of the Securitisation Regulation.
6 (Liquidity)	… manage UK AIFs	Obligations to ensure alignment of investment strategy, liquidity profile and redemption policy of each AIF and (for AIFs other than unleveraged closed-ended AIFs) to employ appropriate liquidity management system and procedures and regularly conduct stress tests.
7 (Risk management)	… manage UK AIFs	Functional and hierarchical separation of risk management from operating units, and setting maximum leverage levels and reporting changes to FCA.[501]

500 For AIFMs that make use of securities financing transactions and total return swaps, the annual reports should include information prescribed under SFTR art. 13.

501 For related FCA powers to take certain measures in order to ensure the stability and integrity of the financial system, see AIFM Regulations r. 68.

8 (Prime brokerage firms)	... manage UK AIFs	Due skill, care and diligence in the selection and appointment of prime brokerage firms; prescribed provisions to be included in prime brokerage firm contracts.
9 (Valuation)	... manage UK AIFs	Valuation of AIF assets and calculation and publication of net asset value.[502]
10 (Delegation)	... manage UK AIFs	Delegation of AIFM management functions, including notifying FCA.[503]
11 (Depositaries)	... manage UK AIFs or market non-UK AIFs in the UK	Appointment of a depositary which carries out (1) all prescribed duties, where the full-scope UK AIFM manages a UK AIF, or (2) a prescribed subset of duties (commonly referred to as "depo-lite") where the full-scope UK AIFM markets a non-UK AIF in the UK.[504]
12 (Marketing a UK AIF in the UK)	... manage UK AIFs	FCA application process for full-scope UK AIFMs wishing to market a UK AIF in the UK.[505]

Additional topics covered in the AIFM Regulations include, most notably:

502 See also AIFM Regulations rr. 24, 25.

503 See also AIFM Regulations rr. 26 to 28.

504 See also AIFM Regulations rr. 29 to 32.

505 See also AIFM Regulations rr. 45 to 64, FUND 10.5 and PERG 8.37.

- management of third country AIFs (including the requirement for appropriate cooperation arrangements to be in place between FCA and supervisory authorities of third country);[506] and

- AIFs which acquire control of non-listed companies and issuers (including notification, disclosure and annual report obligations, and anti asset-stripping restrictions).[507]

In terms of conduct of business rules, the requirements of COBS are significantly modified for full-scope UK AIFMs, as detailed in COBS 18.5A.

13.2.2 Small AIFMs

Small AIFMs are not subject to the supplemental requirements of FUND 3 or the AIFM Regulations.

As with full-scope UK AIFMs, the requirements of COBS are significantly modified for small AIFMs; the modifications are detailed in COBS 18.5.

13.3 Credit Firms

13.3.1 Overview of Supplemental Requirements

The main sourcebook for the supplemental requirements applicable to credit firms is CONC, which is considered in §13.3.2.

CONC brings together and re-codifies many requirements which originated under the predecessor OFT regime, including in national or

[506] AIFM Regulations r. 33. See also FUND 10.4.

[507] AIFM Regulations rr. 34 to 44.

EU legislation,[508] or in guidance that was issued by the OFT.[509] But there are also many others that first appeared in CONC.

In addition, there continues to exist outside of CONC a parallel "black-letter" statutory framework for consumer credit. In particular, regulated credit agreements and regulated consumer hire agreements are governed by many complex statutory requirements imposed by retained provisions of the CCA and connected regulations, which are considered in §13.3.3. Some – but by no means all – of these provisions are cross-referenced in CONC.

Finally, firms should be aware of general consumer rights law – including legislation such as the Consumer Rights Act 2015 (as addressed by the FCA in UNFCOG) and the Consumer Contracts (Information, Cancellation and Additional Charges) Regulations 2013 – which may apply to a firm's consumer credit business. General consumer law is beyond the scope of this book.

13.3.2 CONC Provisions

As stated in CONC 1.1.2G, "*[t]he purpose of CONC is to set out the detailed obligations that are specific to credit-related regulated activities and activities connected to those activities carried on by firms. These build on and add to the high-level obligations, for example, in PRIN, GEN and SYSC, and the requirements in or under the CCA*".

Obligations in CONC that have broad applicability across consumer credit businesses include the following:

---

508 Such as: the CCA and connected regulations; E-Commerce Directive 2000/31/EC; and Financial Services (Distance Marketing) Regulations 2004.

509 Namely: Credit Brokers and Intermediaries Guidance; Debt Collection Guidance; Debt Management (and Credit Repair Services) Guidance; Irresponsible Lending Guidance; Joint Guidance on Payment Protection Products (issued with the FSA); and Mental Capacity Guidance.

Topic	Obligations	CONC ref.
Organisational requirements	Remuneration and performance management	2.11
	Appointment of agents	14
Marketing and treating customers fairly	Financial difficulties	1.3
	Duty not to use misleading names	2.2.3R
	Optional products for which a fee is payable	2.2.6R
	Provision of credit card cheques or unsolicited credit tokens	2.3, 2.9
	Distance marketing, e-commerce	2.7 (including Annex 1 and 2), 2.8
	Mental capacity	2.10
	Meaning of "prominent"; "fair, clear and not misleading" rule (including "buy now pay later")	3.2.3G, 3.3
	Financial promotions about credit agreements not secured on land	3.5
	Financial promotions not in writing	3.10

	Not approving certain financial promotions	3.11
	Calculation of total charge for credit	App 1.1, 1.2

Additional, more detailed obligations in CONC pertaining to specific types of businesses include the following:

Type of Business	Obligations	CONC ref.
Lending and hiring	Use of credit reference agencies by lenders and owners	2.4
	Risk warning for high-cost short-term credit	3.4
	Financial promotions	3.8
	Pre-contractual information, disclosures and conduct	4
	Assessing creditworthiness, needs and circumstances	5.2A
	Cost caps for high-cost short-term credit and rent-to-own agreements	5A, 5B
	Overdrafts	5C, 5D
	Post-contractual requirements	6
	Arrears, default and recovery	7

	Guidance on duty to give information	13
Credit broking	Conduct of business	2.5
	High-cost short-term credit products on price comparison websites	2.5A
	Financial promotions	3.7
	Supplemental conduct of business	5.4
Operating P2P lending electronic system	Financial promotions	3.7A
	Pre-contractual requirements and adequate explanations	4.3
	Creditworthiness assessment	5.5A
	Notices of sums in arrears and default sums	7.17 to 7.19
	Right of withdrawal	11.2
Debt counselling, debt adjusting, providing credit information services	Conduct of business	2.6
	Financial promotions	3.9

	Supplemental conduct of business	8
	Prudential rules for debt management firms	10
Pawn broking	Conduct of business	6.6
Agreements secured on land	Applicability of CONC and MCOB	1.2.7G to 13G
	Financial promotions about credit agreements secured on land	3.6
	Supplemental conduct rules	15.1

13.3.3 CCA Provisions

The CCA enshrines many consumer-protection measures – and corresponding conduct requirements for consumer businesses – in relation to regulated credit and consumer hire agreements.

The version of the CCA now in force is much altered from the one introduced in 1974. Most significantly, a root-and-branch overhaul took place in 2014 when the supervisory jurisdiction for consumer credit was transferred from the Office of Fair Trading ("**OFT**") to the FCA, resulting in the replacement of many long-standing CCA provisions with codified equivalents in FSMA RAO and modules of the FCA Handbook including COBS, SUP and the new CONC. However, much of the CCA survived that great recension and continues to be vital to consumer credit regulation.[510]

Under the CCA, a "**regulated credit agreement**" is, in summary, a credit agreement which (assuming it was entered into on or after 1 April 2014) is not an exempt agreement falling within FSMA RAO arts.60C to 60H.[511]

Similarly, a "**regulated consumer hire agreement**" is, in summary, a consumer hire agreement which (assuming it was entered into on or after 1 April 2014) is not an exempt agreement falling within FSMA RAO

---

510 The FCA recently reviewed whether the retained provisions of the CCA could be repealed and replaced with FCA rules without adversely affect the appropriate degree of protection for consumers (the so-called "statutory question"), but concluded that the scope for doing so is limited by the FCA's inability (under its current rule-making powers) to replicate the consumer protection, statutory sanctions and criminal offences regimes under the CCA. See "Review of retained provisions of the Consumer Credit Act: Final report" (document, 2019).

511 CCA s. 8(3) and FSMA RAO art. 60B(3), supplemented by CONC App 1.3 and 1.4. "**Credit agreement**" is defined in FSMA RAO art. 60B(3) as "*an agreement between an individual or relevant recipient of credit ("A") and any other person ("B") under which B provides A with credit of any amount*" (although the definition is modified in the case of green deal plans). "**Credit**" is defined in art. 60L(1) and CCA s. 9 as including "*a cash loan and any other form of financial accommodation*". A credit agreement entered into before 1 April 2014 is a regulated credit agreement if (1) it was (or became) a regulated agreement within the meaning of CCA s. 189(1) before that date, and (2) would not be an exempt agreement pursuant to art. 60C(2) on 21 March 2016 if the agreement were entered into on that date.

arts.60O to 60Q.[512] Together, regulated credit agreements and regulated consumer hire agreements are referred to as "**regulated agreements**".[513]

Some notable provisions for regulated agreements in the retained CCA are set out below. In certain cases, marked with an asterisk, contravention can render a regulated agreement unenforceable without a court order or until remedied.

---

512 CCA s. 15(2) and FSMA RAO art. 60N(3), supplemented by CONC App 1.4. A "**consumer hire agreement**" is defined in FSMA RAO art. 60N(3)as, generally, "*an agreement between a person ("the owner") and an individual or relevant recipient of credit ("the hirer") for the bailment... of goods to the hirer which (a) is not a hire-purchase agreement, and (b) is capable of subsisting for more than three months*". A consumer hire agreement entered into before 1 April 2014 will be a regulated consumer hire agreement if it was (or became) a regulated agreement within the meaning of CCA s. 189(1) before that date.

513 FCA Handbook Glossary and CCA s. 189(1).

Aspect of Regulated Agreement	**Group of Technical Requirements**	**Legislative ref.**
Prior to contract[514]	Pre-contract disclosure and pre-contract credit information*	CCA s. 55(1); Consumer Credit (Disclosure of Information) Regulations 2004 and 2010[515]
	Canvassing	CCA ss. 48 to 50
	Duty to give copy of draft contract on request	CCA s. 55C
Contract formation	Form, content and signing*	CCA ss. 60, 61; Consumer Credit (Agreements) Regulations 1983 and 2010
	Duty to supply copies*	CCA ss. 61A to 63
	Notice of cancellation rights*	CCA s. 64
	Form and content of securities*	CCA s. 105
	Electronic transmission of documents	CCA s. 176A

514 There are exclusions from pre-contract and contract-formation requirements in ss. 55 to 73 for certain types of agreement, as set out in s. 74.

515 See also CONC 4.2.

Connected lender liability	Liability of creditor for breaches by supplier	CCA ss. 75, 75A
Notifications during lifetime of contract	Duty to give information upon request	CCA ss. 77(1), 78(1), 79(1)[516]
	Statements	CCA ss. 77A, 78(4)
	Notices of sums in arrears or default	CCA ss. 86B to 86E; "Information sheets: consumer credit" (webpage, 2021)
	Information to sureties, debtors and hirers in relation to security*	CCA ss. 107 to 111
Ending of contracts and distress	Procedure on default	CCA ss. 87 to 93
	Rights of withdrawal and cancellation	CCA ss. 66A to 73
	Rights of early payment and termination	CCA ss. 94 to 101
Judicial control	Enforcement orders (providing for the enforceability of regulated agreements notwithstanding infringements of certain requirements including as to pre-contract disclosure and proper execution)	CCA s. 127

516 See also CONC 13.1.

	Time orders (providing for payment by instalments)	CCA s. 129
	Intervention in relation to unfair relationships	CCA ss. 140A to 140C
Ancillary credit business	Prohibition of canvassing certain ancillary credit services off trade premises	CCA ss. 153, 154
	Right to recover brokerage fees if introduction does not result in relevant agreement	CCA s. 155
	Duty of creditor, owner or negotiator to disclose particulars of credit reference agency used	CCA s. 157; Consumer Credit (Conduct of Business) (Credit References) Regulations 1977[517]
	Duty of credit reference agency to disclose filed agency and correct wrong information	CCA ss. 158 to 160; Consumer Credit (Conduct of Business) (Credit References) Regulations 1977
Enforcement	Parallel enforcement duty of the local weights and measures authority (in Great Britain)	CCA s. 161
	Offences, penalties and defences	CCA ss. 167 to 169 and Schedule 1

517 See also CONC 2.4.2R.

EPILOGUE – ON THE HORIZON

Significant regulatory change in UK financial services tends to be well trailed and subject to thorough stakeholder consultation.

Each summer the FCA announces its priorities for the following year in its "Business Plan", twice a year it issues a "Regulatory Initiatives Grid", and since 2019 it has published an annual "Perimeter Report" (which concerns the line between what the FCA does and does not regulate). Proposals that do end up as rule changes are published in final form before coming into force, and can usually be previewed *in situ* using the FCA Handbook's "time travel" functionality.

Some specific regulatory changes on the horizon include:

➢ **Cryptoassets**

The FCA considers that some cryptoassets fall within the regulatory perimeter (broadly, security tokens and e-money tokens) while others do not (utility tokens, exchange tokens).[518] However, even "unregulated" cryptoassets already attract some oversight. In particular, cryptocurrency derivatives can be MiFID financial instruments even where the underlying is not considered to be a currency or commodity, and all cryptoasset exchange providers and custodian wallet providers need to register with the FCA under the MLR.[519] The immediate focus now is on bringing the advertising of all qualifying cryptoassets

518 "Guidance on Cryptoassets – Feedback and Final Guidance to CP 19/3" (PS19/22).

519 "Cryptocurrency derivatives" (webpage, 2018); "Cryptoassets: AML / CTF regime" (webpage, 2021).

(along with other high-risk investments) within the FCA's remit.[520]

➢ **"Buy now pay later"**

In response to the Woolard Review, the FCA is working with the Government to bring "buy now pay later" business (currently exempt from the consumer credit regime) within regulation.[521]

➢ **New "Consumer Duty"**

The FCA proposes to amend PRIN by adding (as a new Principle 12) a "Consumer duty" – namely, "*A firm must act to deliver good outcomes for retail customers*". This would be fleshed out by three "cross cutting obligations" in PRIN 2A.2 and four "retail customer outcomes" in PRIN 2A.3 to 6.[522]

➢ **Wholesale Markets Review**

There are signs that the financial markets can expect to see the first significant divergence of UK onshored regulations from their EU progenitors sooner rather than later. Just a few days after the Brexit implementation period ended, the Short Selling (Notification Thresholds) Regulations 2021 were made, setting a permanent 0.1% threshold and marking a historic break from the 0.2% threshold set by EU law. More recently, certain "quick fixes" were made to the MiFID Org Regulation through the Markets in Financial Instruments (Capital Markets) (Amendment) Regulations 2021, while around the same time

520 "Strengthening our financial promotion rules for high risk investments, including cryptoassets" (CP22/2).

521 "The Woolard Review – A review of change and innovation in the unsecured credit market" (document, 2021); "Regulation of Buy-Now Pay-Later – Consultation" (HM Treasury, 2021).

522 "A new Consumer Duty Feedback to CP21/13 and further consultation" (CP21/36).

the Government also launched a more ambitious consultation on the future of the MiFID-derived wholesale markets framework to consider ways of making the regime simpler and less prescriptive, principally in relation to securities trading obligations.[523]

In addition, there are the big questions – global themes that are driving policy-making in financial services regulation no less than in the wider world:

➢ **ESG**

The FCA states that it supports the Government's roadmap towards net zero carbon emissions and a sustainable economy, and has taken note of its announcement at COP26 that the UK will be the world's first net-zero aligned financial centre. The FCA recognises the role it has to play if these goals are to be attained. On a practical level, this may translate into: "*setting ESG-related expectations at the authorisations gateway; incorporating ESG-related questions and criteria in supervisory assessments and engagements; [and] building ESG-related elements into enforcement models*".[524]

The FCA's ESG strategy currently prioritises the "E" ("environment") strand of ESG owing to the "*scale and urgency of the climate challenge*".[525] More prominence can be expected to be given in due course to the "S" ("social") and "G" ("governance") strands.

➢ **Fourth Industrial Revolution**

Increased automation and interconnectivity bring rapid change, and the delivery of financial services is by its nature highly

523 "Wholesale Markets Review: Consultation" (HM Treasury, 2021).

524 "Climate change and sustainable finance" (webpage, 2021).

525 "A strategy for positive change: our ESG priorities" (webpage, 2021).

susceptible to these forces. In furtherance of its statutory "competition" objective, the FCA has supported the development of fintech by, for example, launching a "regulatory sandbox" in 2016 which had welcomed seven cohorts of "innovative" firms before becoming permanently open in 2021; also in 2021, the FCA ran its first "digital sandbox", which focuses on product or business ideas at an earlier stage of ideation. These two sandboxes, together with future new measures to support partnering between firms and provide support for regulated firms in the growth phase, constitute a putative "scalebox" which has been recommended by a Government-commissioned review into UK fintech.[526] With so much being done to encourage the growth of fintech, financial services providers can be expected to try to achieve more and more with machine learning, artificial intelligence and big data, all of which potentially raise novel risks to customers in terms of fair treatment, positive outcomes and data privacy which might not be adequately addressed by existing regulations.

➢ **Future of Work**

The collective experience of operating through lockdowns and other Covid-19-related disruptions has convinced many (including the FCA – see §5.5) that the future of work for the financial services industry may feature a more dispersed body of staff and decentralised systems and processes. Remote or hybrid working brings an overlay of added risk to many important facets of a firm's operations, including outsourcing resilience, business continuity, cyber and data security and control of inside information, as well as culture and governance. If there is to be a paradigm shift in the way firms typically organise their infrastructure and workforces, FCA expectations and rule-making will need to take that into account.

---

526 "Regulatory sandbox" (webpage, 2021); "Kalifa Review of UK Fintech" (HM Treasury, 2021).

One final question concerns the future of the FCA itself. In the short term, its position looks secure: the Government has repeatedly affirmed its commitment to the UK's "internationally respected" approach to regulation, and is proposing to expand the FCA's and PRA's statutory objectives and regulatory principles as they "*take on greater responsibility for setting detailed rules across a larger portion of the UK's financial services landscape*" as a consequence of Brexit.[527]

Beyond that, much will depend on how successfully the FCA adapts to the new arrangements under which it is answerable to HM Treasury instead of the European Commission and is allocated the whole burden – previously shared with EU institutions – of maintaining the UK's regulatory rulebook.

In addition to meeting these new political and resourcing challenges, the FCA needs to address a systemic vulnerability that has historically afflicted financial regulators generally, and one which was well articulated in a parliamentary note issued during a review of the FCA's predecessor:

> *It is harder to point out the successes of the FSA. This is not because there are none, but simply because they are more of the 'dog that did not bark' variety… There have been some large fines for companies… and yet the benefit of this may never be apparent. Even the evidence can lead to alternative conclusions. Would a large number of heavy fines… indicate that the system was working well or badly?*[528]

Unlike some other regulators, the FCA does not benefit from performance metrics that have "real world" immediacy – trains on time, medical treatments approved, energy bills capped. The FCA's supervisory work, no matter how effective, tends to go unheralded in the press and is disproportionately outweighed by the reputational damage done by perceived "scandals" that happen on its watch. Recently, the collapse of

527 "Financial Services Future Regulatory Framework Review: Proposals for Reform" (HM Treasury, 2021).

528 T. Edmonds, "The Financial Services Authority: looking back, looking forward" (Standard Note SN/BT/3787) (House of Commons Library, 2007).

the LF Woodford Equity Income Fund and mis-selling in relation to British steel pension transfers and London Capital and Finance mini-bonds[529] have brought criticism in the mass media and could yet form part of a pattern that eventually leads to reform of the FCA.

The SIB and FSA each lasted a dozen years, tracing a natural arc of birth, growth, controversy and, finally, replacement, in 2001 and 2013 respectively. The mood music around the Government's ongoing Regulatory Framework Review suggests that the FCA is well placed to break that cycle. But to do so, the FCA will need more than just political goodwill. It will also need resources to match its ever-expanding supervisory responsibilities in a post-Brexit, post-Covid-19, post-COP26 world. And perhaps more challenging, it will need to find something which eluded its forerunners: a way of "pointing out its successes" that resonates with not only financial professionals, but also its paymasters in Government and the man in the street.

---

529 "LF Woodford Equity Income Fund investigation" (webpage, 2021); "FCA statement on British Steel Pension Scheme Redress" (webpage, 2021); "London Capital and Finance plc" (webpage, 2021).

MORE BOOKS BY LAW BRIEF PUBLISHING

A selection of our other titles available now:-

'A Practical Guide to Transgender Law' by Robin Moira White & Nicola Newbegin
'Artificial Intelligence – The Practical Legal Issues (2nd Edition)' by John Buyers
'A Practical Guide to Challenging Sham Marriage Allegations in Immigration Law' by Priya Solanki
'A Practical Guide to New Build Conveyancing' by Paul Sams & Rebecca East
'A Practical Guide to Inherited Wealth on Divorce' by Hayley Trim
'A Practical Guide to Shareholder Disputes in Family Businesses' by Ed Weeks
'A Practical Guide to the Law of Forests in Scotland' by Philip Buchan
'A Practical Guide to Health and Medical Cases in Immigration Law' by Rebecca Chapman & Miranda Butler
'A Practical Guide to Bad Character Evidence for Criminal Practitioners by Aparna Rao
'A Practical Guide to Environmental Enforcement' by Christopher Badger & Stuart Jessop
'A Practical Guide to Hoarding and Mental Health for Housing Lawyers' by Rachel Coyle
'A Practical Guide to Psychiatric Claims in Personal Injury – 2nd Edition' by Liam Ryan
'Stephens on Contractual Indemnities' by Richard Stephens
'A Practical Guide to the EU Succession Regulation' by Richard Frimston
'A Practical Guide to Solicitor and Client Costs – 2nd Edition' by Robin Dunne
'Constructive Dismissal – Practice Pointers and Principles' by Benjimin Burgher
'A Practical Guide to Religion and Belief Discrimination Claims in the Workplace' by Kashif Ali
'A Practical Guide to the Law of Medical Treatment Decisions' by Ben Troke

'Fundamental Dishonesty and QOCS in Personal Injury Proceedings: Law and Practice' by Jake Rowley
'A Practical Guide to the Law in Relation to School Exclusions' by Charlotte Hadfield & Alice de Coverley
'A Practical Guide to Divorce for the Silver Separators' by Karin Walker
'The Right to be Forgotten – The Law and Practical Issues' by Melissa Stock
'A Practical Guide to Planning Law and Rights of Way in National Parks, the Broads and AONBs' by James Maurici QC, James Neill et al
'A Practical Guide to Election Law' by Tom Tabori
'A Practical Guide to the Law in Relation to Surrogacy' by Andrew Powell
'A Practical Guide to Claims Arising from Fatal Accidents – 2nd Edition' by James Patience
'A Practical Guide to the Ownership of Employee Inventions – From Entitlement to Compensation' by James Tumbridge & Ashley Roughton
'A Practical Guide to Asbestos Claims' by Jonathan Owen & Gareth McAloon
'A Practical Guide to Stamp Duty Land Tax in England and Northern Ireland' by Suzanne O'Hara
'A Practical Guide to the Law of Farming Partnerships' by Philip Whitcomb
'Covid-19, Homeworking and the Law – The Essential Guide to Employment and GDPR Issues' by Forbes Solicitors
'Covid-19, Force Majeure and Frustration of Contracts – The Essential Guide' by Keith Markham
'Covid-19 and Criminal Law – The Essential Guide' by Ramya Nagesh
'Covid-19 and Family Law in England and Wales – The Essential Guide' by Safda Mahmood
'A Practical Guide to the Law of Unlawful Eviction and Harassment – 2nd Edition' by Stephanie Lovegrove
'Covid-19, Residential Property, Equity Release and Enfranchisement – The Essential Guide' by Paul Sams and Louise Uphill
'Covid-19, Brexit and the Law of Commercial Leases – The Essential Guide' by Mark Shelton
'A Practical Guide to Costs in Personal Injury Claims – 2nd Edition' by Matthew Hoe

‘A Practical Guide to the General Data Protection Regulation (GDPR) – 2nd Edition’ by Keith Markham

‘Ellis on Credit Hire – Sixth Edition’ by Aidan Ellis & Tim Kevan

‘A Practical Guide to Working with Litigants in Person and McKenzie Friends in Family Cases’ by Stuart Barlow

‘Protecting Unregistered Brands: A Practical Guide to the Law of Passing Off’ by Lorna Brazell

‘A Practical Guide to Secondary Liability and Joint Enterprise Post-Jogee’ by Joanne Cecil & James Mehigan

‘A Practical Guide to the Pre-Action RTA Claims Protocol for Personal Injury Lawyers’ by Antonia Ford

‘A Practical Guide to Neighbour Disputes and the Law’ by Alexander Walsh

‘A Practical Guide to Forfeiture of Leases’ by Mark Shelton

‘A Practical Guide to Coercive Control for Legal Practitioners and Victims’ by Rachel Horman

‘A Practical Guide to Rights Over Airspace and Subsoil’ by Daniel Gatty

‘Tackling Disclosure in the Criminal Courts – A Practitioner’s Guide’ by Narita Bahra QC & Don Ramble

‘A Practical Guide to the Law of Driverless Cars – Second Edition’ by Alex Glassbrook, Emma Northey & Scarlett Milligan

‘A Practical Guide to TOLATA Claims’ by Greg Williams

‘A Practical Guide to Elderly Law – 2nd Edition’ by Justin Patten

‘A Practical Guide to the Law of Prescription in Scotland’ by Andrew Foyle

‘A Practical Guide to the Construction and Rectification of Wills and Trust Instruments’ by Edward Hewitt

‘A Practical Guide to the Law of Bullying and Harassment in the Workplace’ by Philip Hyland

‘How to Be a Freelance Solicitor: A Practical Guide to the SRA-Regulated Freelance Solicitor Model’ by Paul Bennett

‘A Practical Guide to Prison Injury Claims’ by Malcolm Johnson

‘A Practical Guide to the Small Claims Track - 2nd Edition’ by Dominic Bright

‘A Practical Guide to Advising Clients at the Police Station’ by Colin Stephen McKeown-Beaumont

'A Practical Guide to Antisocial Behaviour Injunctions' by Iain Wightwick
'Practical Mediation: A Guide for Mediators, Advocates, Advisers, Lawyers, and Students in Civil, Commercial, Business, Property, Workplace, and Employment Cases' by Jonathan Dingle with John Sephton
'The Mini-Pupillage Workbook' by David Boyle
'A Practical Guide to Crofting Law' by Brian Inkster
'A Practical Guide to Spousal Maintenance' by Liz Cowell
'A Practical Guide to the Law of Domain Names and Cybersquatting' by Andrew Clemson
'A Practical Guide to the Law of Gender Pay Gap Reporting' by Harini Iyengar
'A Practical Guide to the Rights of Grandparents in Children Proceedings' by Stuart Barlow
'NHS Whistleblowing and the Law' by Joseph England
'Employment Law and the Gig Economy' by Nigel Mackay & Annie Powell
'A Practical Guide to Noise Induced Hearing Loss (NIHL) Claims' by Andrew Mckie, Ian Skeate, Gareth McAloon
'An Introduction to Beauty Negligence Claims – A Practical Guide for the Personal Injury Practitioner' by Greg Almond
'Intercompany Agreements for Transfer Pricing Compliance' by Paul Sutton
'Zen and the Art of Mediation' by Martin Plowman
'A Practical Guide to the SRA Principles, Individual and Law Firm Codes of Conduct 2019 – What Every Law Firm Needs to Know' by Paul Bennett
'A Practical Guide to Adoption for Family Lawyers' by Graham Pegg
'A Practical Guide to Industrial Disease Claims' by Andrew Mckie & Ian Skeate
'A Practical Guide to Redundancy' by Philip Hyland
'A Practical Guide to Vicarious Liability' by Mariel Irvine
'A Practical Guide to Applications for Landlord's Consent and Variation of Leases' by Mark Shelton
'A Practical Guide to Relief from Sanctions Post-Mitchell and Denton' by Peter Causton
'A Practical Guide to Equity Release for Advisors' by Paul Sams
'A Practical Guide to Financial Services Claims' by Chris Hegarty

'The Law of Houses in Multiple Occupation: A Practical Guide to HMO Proceedings' by Julian Hunt
'Occupiers, Highways and Defective Premises Claims: A Practical Guide Post-Jackson – 2nd Edition' by Andrew Mckie
'A Practical Guide to Financial Ombudsman Service Claims' by Adam Temple & Robert Scrivenor
'A Practical Guide to Advising Schools on Employment Law' by Jonathan Holden
'A Practical Guide to Running Housing Disrepair and Cavity Wall Claims: 2nd Edition' by Andrew Mckie & Ian Skeate
'A Practical Guide to Holiday Sickness Claims – 2nd Edition' by Andrew Mckie & Ian Skeate
'Arguments and Tactics for Personal Injury and Clinical Negligence Claims' by Dorian Williams
'A Practical Guide to Drone Law' by Rufus Ballaster, Andrew Firman, Eleanor Clot
'A Practical Guide to Compliance for Personal Injury Firms Working With Claims Management Companies' by Paul Bennett
'RTA Allegations of Fraud in a Post-Jackson Era: The Handbook – 2nd Edition' by Andrew Mckie
'RTA Personal Injury Claims: A Practical Guide Post-Jackson' by Andrew Mckie
'On Experts: CPR35 for Lawyers and Experts' by David Boyle
'An Introduction to Personal Injury Law' by David Boyle
'A Practical Guide to Subtle Brain Injury Claims' by Pankaj Madan

These books and more are available to order online direct from the publisher at www.lawbriefpublishing.com, where you can also read free sample chapters. For any queries, contact us on 0844 587 2383 or mail@lawbriefpublishing.com.

Our books are also usually in stock at www.amazon.co.uk with free next day delivery for Prime members, and at good legal bookshops such as Wildy & Sons.

We are regularly launching new books in our series of practical day-to-day practitioners' guides. Visit our website and join our free newsletter to be kept informed and to receive special offers, free chapters, etc.

You can also follow us on Twitter at www.twitter.com/lawbriefpub.

www.ingramcontent.com/pod-product-compliance
Lightning Source LLC
LaVergne TN
LVHW052303200926
848481LV00002B/449
9781914608384